Animal Patients
50 Years in the Life
of an Animal Doctor

Edward J. Scanlon, V.M.D.

with Martha Scanlon Ronemus

Camino Books, Inc.
Philadelphia

To all my family, past and present, especially my four daughters, four grandchildren, and one great-grandson.

Manufactured in the United States of America

1 2 3 4 5 04 03 02 01 00

Library of Congress Cataloging-in-Publication Data

Scanlon, Edward J.
    Animal Patients / 50 years in the life of an animal doctor / Edward J. Scanlon with Martha Scanlon Ronemus.
        p.   cm.
    ISBN 0-940159-65-1 (paperback : alk. paper)
    1. Scanlon, Edward J. 2. Veterinarians—Pennsylvania—Philadelphia—Anecdotes. 3. Cats—Pennsylvania—Philadelphia—Anecdotes. 4. Dogs—Pennsylvania—Philadelphia—Anecdotes. 5. Veterinary medicine—Pennsylvania—Philadelphia—Anecdotes. I. Ronemus, Martha Scanlon. II. Title.

SF613.S29 A3 2000
636.089'092—dc21   99-38248

Published in conjunction with Middle Atlantic Press

For information write:

Camino Books, Inc.
P. O. Box 59026
Philadelphia, PA 19102

www.caminobooks.com

Contents

one

Night Unto Day

It has always been part of the endless fascination of my profession that life seems to come full circle; fate will often hand us an unhappy, painful situation, followed by a gratifying, happy experience. Maybe the Fates mean us to be kept a little off-balance. Two cases, very early in my career, come to mind. They were in turn humbling and elating.

There were many times during my forty-two years as a practicing veterinarian when I wondered how I had gotten myself into an uncomfortable fix, but for near-panic and apprehension, none surpassed the time I found myself in the garage of one of Pennsylvania's premier judges, watching the body of his once-proud Doberman pinscher being wrapped in a pink blanket and shipped off for autopsy. About an hour earlier, I had pronounced the dog healthy and perfect, and now I stood accused of being a butcher and a canine killer. How could this have happened?

I had been in practice only a short while and had missed

the yearly opportunity for a listing in the telephone book. Back in 1946, it was considered unethical to advertise, so my only source of clients, apart from those who happened to notice my shingle as they went by, was recommendations from satisfied owners.

It was a slow way to build a practice, and I had only a few appointments each day. It seemed that the least I could do was give every dog or cat—as well as the occasional rabbit, guinea pig, turtle, or caged bird—my undivided attention. I considered myself lucky, though, because I was young, strong, eager to succeed, and I had a secret weapon—Mrs. Walsh.

I had inherited the incomparable Mrs. Walsh from my mentor, Dr. Otto Stader, when he gave up his practice. She was not only efficient to the point of obsession, she was the perfect veterinary office manager. She knew how to be sympathetic when a pet died or the prognosis wasn't good, and she greeted the arrival of a new animal in a household with the enthusiasm some women would have reserved for a new baby. She also was part of the elite social world of the Main Line of Philadelphia, where I had started my practice. Although she had been forced to work upon the death of her husband, she knew and socialized with many of the finest families in the area. She was one of them.

Physically thin, typical of the closet drinker whose calories come from alcohol rather than from food, she had excellent patrician features, with sympathetic blue eyes. Her colored hair was always cut in the latest style, and she carried her more-than-average height well. She had a wry sense of the absurd and a clever way of looking at things that helped keep the days on an even keel.

She also had one of the most highly developed passions for gossip that I have ever encountered, before or since. She turned my waiting room into a secret intelligence office, persuading clients to make all sorts of indiscreet revelations, storing all tidbits in her encyclopedic mind. Her interrogation techniques could have set the pattern for police the world around, as no one she questioned seemed to know how much they were revealing.

"Oh, you live on Oak Lane," she might say to a client. "We have another patient there, Mr. Johnson's little dog, Spot." This would, of course, draw out all sorts of goodies about the Johnsons.

Her best, though, was her exasperated "Oh, MEN!" with eyes rolled toward the ceiling. There was something about the way she said it that would bring forth any number of revelations about the client's own man and any other man who had done anything of note recently, whether good or bad.

She actually kept the Social Directory, Who's Who, the List of Daughters of the American Revolution, and other such books in her desk drawer for handy reference. There was little concerning any client that she didn't know—or couldn't find out. Her compulsion to know all, however, never got her in trouble, and I was often grateful for the knowledge when I was obliged to make small talk with someone while examining their pet. The squeamish ones needed all the distraction one could provide. Although I could ill afford her at that stage in my career, I was lucky to have such an experienced and competent woman at the front desk.

Most physicians dislike being interrupted while they are with patients, and veterinarians are no exception. I probably disliked it more than most because my patients were so few. So when Mrs. Walsh interrupted my examination of a sweet, oddly marked tabby cat named Lucy, I knew something unusual was going on.

"It's Mrs. Allesandroni," she said.

Mrs. Allesandroni's new five-month-old Doberman pinscher had been the only other patient of the morning. Mrs. Allesandroni and her daughter had brought the pup in, both women wearing expensive clothing and looking elegant and composed. The dog's natural aristocratic bearing was a perfect complement to theirs. I had vaccinated the dog with a distemper booster and given the owners dietary advice, and had arranged for future lab work to check for worms and give a rabies vaccine. I thought she was probably just calling about some question she had forgotten while she was in the office, but Mrs. Walsh's tone of voice banished that thought. "You'd better take it now." The urgency in her voice made me gulp.

"You incompetent butcher! You killer!" Mrs. Allesandroni greeted me. The butcher part had some truth to it—one of the ironies of my life is that I was employed as a meat cutter while working my way through college to become a vet. It was, however, startling to hear the patrician judge's wife calling me a killer.

"My dog's dying. He's collapsed on the garage floor and he can hardly breathe. He's messing everywhere. I'm calling the judge. You told me my dog was perfect less than an hour ago—you told me he was an exceptionally fine pup. He was fine until you gave him that injection."

My blood pressure rose as soon as I heard the symptoms. I heard a rushing sound in my ears as all thought turned to wordless pre-panic. Mrs. Allesandroni had perfectly described a dog in extremis—dying. The labored, irregular respiration, collapse, involuntary passage of urine and feces were all terminal signs. I interrupted her tirade to say I would be there as quickly as I could drive and hung up the phone.

I nearly threw poor Lucy, the cat I was examining, into her metal carrier. "Mrs. Thompson, an emergency's come up," I said, all the while praying she hadn't overheard Mrs. Allesandroni's accusations of malpractice. "I'll have to finish Lucy's physical later. Mrs. Walsh will give you another appointment, at no charge."

I grabbed my black medical bag, typical for back then—a graduation gift still shiny with lack of use—and started for Judges' Row. Philadelphia judges were required to be city residents, and they were clustered in one area within a few blocks of each other near City Line Avenue: Vincent A. Carroll, president of the Friendly Sons of St. Patrick, who led the St. Patrick's Day parade astride a white horse; "Hanging"

Harry McDevitt, known for giving five-year sentences for petty theft; and Judge Eugene Allesandroni, known for presiding over some of Philadelphia's biggest cases, were all neighbors.

As I sped toward the Allesandronis' home, I reviewed the details of the case. Mrs. Allesandroni had brought the dog in not only for its booster shots but to have it given a certificate of health. She had purchased the dog contingent on its passing a vet's exam. I remembered, with a shudder, complimenting her on acquiring such a healthy and handsome animal. "He should be, for the money they're asking," was Mrs. Allesandroni's reply. Her concern for finances had seemed a bit cold, but I knew her to be a caring mistress to the family's other dog, a female Doberman named Delilah. The new male pup had been named, predictably, Samson.

Judge Allesandroni was frequently mentioned in Philadelphia papers, and always with regard to his reputation for fairness, integrity, and superior knowledge of the law. I had met him only once, when he and his wife had brought Delilah in for an appointment. He had scrutinized me for several moments, then pronounced, "Darn if you aren't the image of your father." I had no grounds to dispute his words; my father had died when I was only three, my mother in a flu epidemic two years before him. I had no real recollections of them.

He went on to explain that he and my father had shared a rented room in Harrisburg while taking the state bar exams immediately following graduation from Penn's law school. Neither had been able to afford a single room for the several days of exams, so one would study while the other slept; then they would switch.

"So you decided to bypass the law?" he asked. I explained that I had never felt drawn to the law. "Your dad was a fine attorney," the judge said, more a statement than a question of the wisdom of my career choice.

I hoped his reputation for fairness and integrity was deserved. If it wasn't, I could be in for a lot of trouble!

Pulling into the driveway, I bypassed the large English Tudor house and headed straight for the detached garage, where I could see a cluster of people. In addition to Mrs. Allesandroni and a woman in a maid's uniform and apron, there was also their stunning daughter, Angelica, who was a recent graduate of the University of Pennsylvania and as intelligent as she was lovely.

Next to a shining black limousine, the dog was lying in a pool of urine, his hind end covered with feces, while an ever-widening pool of saliva dripped from his open jaws. All testified to the dog's complete loss of control over his own body. As soon as Mrs. Allesandroni saw me, she resumed the attack she had begun over the phone, repeating, "You said he was perfect," as though by saying it enough, she could make it so.

Fitting my stethoscope into my ears provided momentary relief, but I could well imagine what she was saying. Concentrating on the patient before me, I could see Samson was literally breathing his last. My experience with school, my first job at the SPCA, and my internship with the world-renowned Dr. Otto Stader served only to separate me from any false hopes; it would take a miracle to save this dog's life, and none would be forthcoming. As Samson let out his final large exhalation, the so-called death rattle, I started rhythmically compressing his chest, futilely going through the motions of artificial respiration. Stopping briefly, I reached into my black bag and withdrew a syringe, preloaded with cardiac stimulant. I put the needle directly into the dog's heart and pushed the plunger. I had performed this intracardial injection many times, but for different reasons, at the SPCA, and now, as in most cases, it was futile.

By now, Mrs. Allesandroni was nearly screaming, "He's dead, he's dead, you killer!" This was most unnerving.

I don't know what I would have done next, and thankfully I was saved by the bell—the phone bell. The entire situation was made even more intimidating by the fact that I was actually in a place where they had telephones in the garage. Remember, this was 1946.

Angelica picked it up and haltingly but concisely described the situation to "Daddy." She then gave the phone to her mother, who gave her version of the tragedy. "I want this killer punished! His injection at the office did it. Samson was perfect before, he was perfect!"

Trying to keep my composure, I asked if I could speak with the judge. I explained to him that the vaccine I had used was very safe and had been used on many other dogs with no problems. There was the possibility of an allergy, though Samson's reaction wasn't typical of that. "Please let me send him to the veterinary school for a postmortem. Without a post, we'll just be guessing."

Mrs. Allesandroni overheard my request and proclaimed, "I won't allow it! You'll just send him to a friend, someone who will cover up for you. I know how it is."

Her husband heard her in the background and directed me to put her on. I gathered from her side of the conversation that the judge proposed the dog be sent to the school for autopsy via taxi, under his name. As my name would not be connected with the dog in any way, her fears of a conspiracy would be allayed.

Angelica intervened in my behalf, to a silent chorus of thanks from me. "Mother, that's the only fair thing to do. After all, you've always been pleased with Dr. Scanlon's work with Delilah. You've even recommended him to friends. He deserves the benefit of the doubt. We just can't leave things this way."

Between her husband's and her daughter's words, Mrs. Allesandroni calmed down and agreed. Allowing her practical side to take over, she began issuing orders to the maid. "Get a blanket to wrap him in, and have the gardener put him in my car. There's no need for a taxi. I'll write a note on the judge's stationery, telling the postmortem department that they'll report directly to him."

Without sparing me a glance, she turned her back and marched into the house. I was going to have a tough time getting back into her good graces. She had already made up her mind about my guilt and didn't want to be confused by anything like facts.

I stayed in the garage while the dog's body was wrapped in a pink blanket and placed in the back seat of the limo. After I had failed to save his life, it seemed the least I could do. Mixed in with my sadness over the loss of such a fine young dog was my worry about what this could mean for my career. My wife and I were expecting our first baby, and practice growth depended upon my keeping animals alive and healthy. Having someone as influential as Mrs. Allesandroni spreading the word that I was a butcher and a murderer didn't bode well. Everything depended on the results of the postmortem.

After a night devoted to worrying rather than to rest, I went to my clinic and spent the morning jumping every time the phone rang. Finally, Mrs. Walsh announced the call from Judge Allesandroni.

"Dr. Scanlon, good morning. I just received a call from Dr. Martin." Dr. Martin was the head of pathology at the University of Pennsylvania's School of Veterinary Medicine. "His examination of Samson determined that the death was caused by a ruptured aortic aneurysm and was probably a birth defect. He explained to me that it was undetectable with the normal physical examination."

I resisted an impulse to let out a cheer and allowed myself only a sigh of relief.

The judge adopted a kindly, almost fatherly tone. "Now, I've talked to my wife. I'll admit she does get carried away sometimes, but she accepts the findings, and I think feels a little guilty about how she treated you. She knows now the dog would have died sooner or later, and she said to tell you that when we get a new puppy, we will of course bring it to you for care."

Somehow I managed to say good-bye without sacrificing too much dignity. If he had been there in person, I would have had to resist the impulse to kiss the hem of his black robe. I ran into the waiting room to tell Mrs. Walsh the good news, for once glad of my lack of patients. It wouldn't do much for their confidence to see their vet dancing with joy at the judge's verdict—innocent of puppycide.

Two days after the Samson tragedy, fate offered me an unusually happy case.

The Lower Merion Animal Control officer, better known as the dog catcher, brought me a kitten around five months old. Officer Bill Ivens wore a neat uniform, polished boots, and a concerned expression. "I don't know if you can help him or not." His strong hands gently placed a prone calico (tri-color) kitten on the exam table. "He sure is out of it."

"All tri-color cats are female, Bill. What's the story? What happened to her?"

"Don't know. I was driving east on Montgomery Avenue and saw her under some bushes on the west side. Swung around, picked her up, and here we are. She could be a stray or maybe somebody dumped her." He shook his head. "They do that, you know." I liked his obvious concern. His job often breeds a callous person.

My examination revealed slowed but steady aspirations. There were no external marks anywhere on her body, no grease stains or abrasions typical of car accidents. No bite marks or broken bones. Her heart action, like the respirations, was slow but steady. The pupillary reflexes were poor. There was a small area on the right side of the kitten's head, just below her ear and above the eye, that was missing hair. The area was beginning to swell with a bluish discoloration.

"It seems we have a very nasty concussion, Bill. It's unusual that there are no areas of damage except for her head. Fortunate, though."

Officer Bill leaned over and looked at the kitten's head. "What do you think? Can you save her?"

"These cases are always touch and go for the first twenty-four to forty-eight hours. It was caused by a glancing blow of some kind, probably a car. As I said, the absence of signs of

abdominal and chest damage is in our favor." The little creature on my table was winsome. Her face was covered with tiny
black spots, looking like freckles. She was steady under my
hands, purring as injured cats often do. I found myself rooting
for her recovery in a personal, as well as professional, way.
Somehow I felt there was a connection between the courageous little feline and me.

I picked out a hypodermic syringe from the sterilizer. (This
was long before the day of the disposable syringe. Much effort
and time went into keeping equipment pristine.) I explained,
"We'll start treatment and I'll monitor her closely the rest of
the day and tonight if necessary. Cross your fingers."

Carefully untying a pink and lavender ribbon from the kitten's neck, I handed it to the officer. "Now it's your turn, Bill.
See if you can find her owner."

He frowned. "Sometimes we find them. Sometimes they
find us. Sometimes they go to the SPCA."

Veterinarians handle stray cases, ownerless pets, or wild
animals in various ways. A few will give minimum or little
treatment and "pass the buck" to the SPCA. At the very beginning, I decided that such cases should be treated as though
they all had responsible and loving owners. No short cuts. If
they needed X-rays, blood transfusions, surgery, or expensive
drugs, they received them. That was my policy from day one
until retirement over forty years later. Of course, I hoped to be
compensated, hoped that an owner would be found.

Missy Calico, as I dubbed the ownerless kitten, was a
sweetheart, medically speaking and personality-wise. Within
a day, she was in control of 90 percent or better of her senses,
eating and purring up a storm. Bill reported, "We have had no
inquiries, no clues as to an owner. I think she may have been
thrown out of a car. Some SOBs do that. But I'll keep you informed."

Early on the third day, with no hint of an owner, I was beginning to get a little nervous. Missy Calico was such a sweet,
good-looking kitten and would be just an ideal pet. She loved

to play and had obviously been given considerable attention. The pink ribbon showed someone cared. I was even beginning to entertain thoughts of taking her home with me, but that would not be a good precedent. I could just imagine what life would be like if I became attached to, and took home, every ownerless animal.

Late that afternoon, Officer Bill called. "Doc, some people are on their way over to see the kitten. Sounds like it might be theirs, from the description."

What happened next was a happy ending, worthy of Frank Capra's *It's a Wonderful Life* movie, and almost too good to be true. It shows that life does indeed imitate art. Into my waiting room came a lovely young girl, perhaps nine or ten years old. She had to be pushed into the waiting room in a wheelchair by an attentive man who turned out to be her father.

"Oh, Doctor," the words rushed out, "I hope you have my kitten, my Birthday Lady. They said she was hurt and might be here." She looked at me with eyes brimming with tears, but then seemed to remember her manners. "My name is Helga Larson, and this is my father."

"Did she wear a pink ribbon with a lavender bow?" I asked.

"Yes! Yes! Is she all right?" Helga was now dabbing tears and speaking through faintly trembling lips. Her father, with a comforting, bracing arm about her shoulders, looked apprehensive.

"Your Birthday Lady is fine, Helga. She is just about completely recovered and ready to take home." I felt and swallowed a very small lump. The gratitude and joy in the girl's innocent blue eyes was moving. She brushed aside her light brown, braided hair and wiped her cheeks.

Her father sighed. "Thank heavens, and thank you, Doctor. We were afraid we had lost her. We left her in the care of a teenage neighbor while I took Helga to a Baltimore specialist. We had to stay overnight." His grimace left much unsaid. He questioned, "Do you board pets? We have a few more Baltimore visits to make."

Looking toward Helga, I answered, "Your Birthday Lady is welcome anytime. We'll reserve the pink and lavender suite for her. How about that?"

The now dry-eyed Helga and her smiling father listened attentively to my after-care instructions. After concluding, I asked, "So, Helga, your kitten was a birthday present?"

"Yes, and the best and most wonderful ever." Looking at her father, "Not that Daddy doesn't always give me the greatest presents, but Birthday Lady, well, she's special. My nanny loves her too, and will be so happy to see her."

As soon as they departed, I called Officer Bill. "Bingo," was all I said after identifying myself.

"It's great to win one now and then, eh, Doc?" A pause. "It couldn't have happened to nicer people. Helga was in a bad car accident; her mother was killed. The kid has had a rough time."

Cradling the phone, I smiled and reflected. Officer Bill was really pleased. Helga was ecstatic. Her father and the nanny were happy. Birthday Lady, fully restored, was probably playing joyfully with her mistress and certainly wearing a new neck ribbon.

What a gratifying, satisfying ending. What a great day!

two

Getting There
Is Half the Fun

I have often been asked, "Why did you become a veterinarian?" Sometimes it is a simple question, asked out of honest curiosity, but other times I hear the implicit addition, "instead of choosing medicine, law, or dentistry, a REAL profession?"

I certainly didn't become an animal doctor for the money or the prestige. In the mid-1940s, when I started practicing, most vets were given little more respect than blacksmiths (who, by the way, are finally enjoying due credit for their knowledge and ability). The fees were small—only two dollars for an office call!—and often grudgingly paid. There was no health insurance for pets then. (Even today, little is available.) Though the education was (and is) comparable to a physician's both in time and in cost, then, as now, far more money could be made treating human ills.

I chose veterinary medicine because, pure and simple, I loved and enjoyed working with animals. And even today, after having cared for thousands, I have endless curiosity and wonder at their variety. The horse still fascinates me, ranging from the hardworking, 2,200-pound Percheron to the little 200-pound Shetland pony, meeting in the middle with the half-ton Thoroughbred. It still makes my heart beat faster to watch one run, especially if it comes in first and I have money on it! Even their many coat colors—flashy chestnut, dull dun, roan, palomino—have a fascination. Sheep, goats, cattle, and much-maligned swine all have their own secrets.

I have a special fondness for family pets. When I first started my practice I saw dogs almost exclusively. As time went by I saw more and more cats, plus the "exotics." When I first began, I never dreamed I would treat a pot-bellied pig or an emu—who could have imagined it!

To me, all animals are wondrous. Learning their habits, needs, and characteristics is an endlessly captivating pursuit. Finding the secrets of diagnosing their diseases and learning to prevent and cure them is a daunting task, but the only one that ever interested me. Yes, I knew what I wanted to do with my life. I was going to be a veterinarian, and nothing was going to stop me. Getting the needed preparation, though, was going to require some very hard work on my part, and I was going to learn some of my most important lessons in life during that period.

Veterinary medicine is actually one of the more difficult fields of study. Then, as now, there were more applicants per available spot than for any other postgraduate course, including human medicine. At the time I studied, there were only about twenty schools in the United States that offered a veterinary degree. The University of Pennsylvania was the most prestigious, and I wanted to be graduated from that program with its deserved fame. The Penn program was preeminent and enjoyed worldwide acclaim. Interestingly enough, Penn, unlike nearby Cornell, didn't give first preference to state residents. They had a contract to accept a number from the New England states, where there was no accredited program, and they took top applicants from other states (my class contained three Californians, two Virginians, and a Marylander). Penn also leaned toward those with rural backgrounds, since significant funding came from the state and federal departments of agriculture. Applicants from Pennsylvania were aware of the poor odds for admission. I thought perhaps I was chosen as a token minority—a city boy, with modest scholastic grades from a Catholic-administered college. Regardless, I was overjoyed at being selected!

By 1999, over 60 percent of the applicants accepted into Penn's veterinary medicine program were women, and I believe veterinary medicine will eventually become a predominantly female profession. In my day, women were the exception. The prevailing opinion was that women were in college to find a husband, would work only part time if at all, and couldn't handle the physical requirements of a large-animal practice. This seems ridiculous now, but in the 1940s, Penn was considered very radical: there were two women in my class.

Before I could even apply, though, the first big hurdle was acquiring the necessary college credits. At that time, two years of college were required before admission to vet school. It soon went up to four years. Upon my graduation from high school in 1936, it was understood that I was going to have to pay for my own education. Student loans from the government were somewhere in the future. I considered myself fortunate to have the opportunity to work my way through college. Some of the jobs I had gave me as much of an education as the university did.

Through a family friend, I was able to get a job at the DuPont paint manufacturing plant in Philadelphia as a janitor and elevator operator. The job paid well and was a good opportunity to save money. With any luck, after a year or two of saving, I would be able to start college. However, I hid my plans to go on to college and vet school in order to get the job. DuPont liked to promote from within the plant, and I feared that the company wouldn't want a worker who would quit after a year.

I didn't remain a janitor for long. After a few months I was moved up to the top floor as a mixer. The pay was better, but the noise on the floor was deafening. Maybe that's why barking dogs never bother me. I know this helped me learn to concentrate amidst chaos.

Several months later, through a little luck, hard work, and some seniority, I was offered a job in the research laboratory. I quickly accepted. The large laboratory building employed fifteen to twenty chemists, each with his own small lab, an office, and an assistant or "stooge," as the assistants were universally called. The stooges didn't have chemists' degrees, but it was a higher-paying, more prestigious position. I was assigned to be stooge for Dr. Roy Davis, a tall, handsome man I was told was "going places." Roy was a natural diplomat. He was smart and articulate, and he treated everyone as an equal—even his inferiors. (Another lesson!)

This was a different world from the manufacturing side. I associated with doctors of chemistry and heard about and saw their exciting experiments. I came to work in a shirt and tie, rather than paint-stained coveralls. This job was not connected to my ambitions, but it was stimulating compared to janitorial work and mixing paint. Most of the assistants felt they had a future with DuPont. A high school diploma was required, and a lot of us took college courses at night, many working toward the chemistry degree. There were no promises, but we knew we had the inside track toward promotions to higher positions in other plants. With my hidden agenda, I felt like an impostor within the fraternity of Company men.

Roy did go places—to the Wilmington headquarters, to be exact. Rumor had it that he got the promotion only because he "married right"—to the daughter of a highly placed DuPont executive. That couldn't have hurt, but it was an unfair judgment. Roy was imbued with natural talent and intelligence. His parting words had a sting—"Ed, keep doing the job right. I have a feeling we'll be working together in the future." I thanked him sincerely for his show of confidence in me, but

I knew that if we did work together again, it would be because I had failed in my true goal.

I heard from Roy again when I announced my intention to leave DuPont and go to college full time to earn my pre-vet credits. He called to tell me not to do anything until we had had a chance to meet. "I want to see you for lunch Saturday. Don't do anything until we talk."

I was his guest at the Hotel du Pont in Wilmington, still one of the loveliest "old world"–style hotels on the East Coast. He had come with an array of facts and figures to support his case. "I've been looking into the veterinary profession, and I was wondering if you realize the average vet's income isn't much more than you're making now. And you still have a long way to go with DuPont. A lot of guys, myself included, think you could make it big in sales."

Roy was sacrificing his precious leisure time to keep me from making what he saw as a major career mistake, and I was touched. I was giving up a good job in an up-and-coming industry for an unknown future in a profession that, with all the changes in farming, seemed to be on the way out. To a practical man like Roy Davis, it must have seemed like insanity. Still, I tried to explain my hopes and ambitions. "It isn't a matter of money. It's what I've always wanted to do. It's something I *have* to do."

When he recognized that I wouldn't be swayed, he said, "Do one thing. Don't resign. Ask for an educational leave of absence instead. The company will pick up the tab for your chemistry classes, and if things don't work out, you can come back." As far as I know, I'm still on leave of absence from DuPont. I confess that on occasion, usually when under severe financial stress, I have wondered where I'd be if I had stayed on at DuPont. I'm sure the executives and higher-ups are way ahead of me in money, but I can't imagine how bereft of satisfaction my life would have been if I hadn't followed my vocation.

The two years I spent at La Salle College (now a university), acquiring my pre-vet credits, were fairly easy years. I had no serious financial problems and was, in fact, able to save considerable money toward vet school. The Penn Fruit Company, a supermarket operator of that era, had an opening for an apprentice meat cutter, and I was hired. It was a dream job. Without that good fortune I never could have made it. It was, however, a two-way street. The company didn't have to carry me as a full-time employee although I always worked forty or more hours per week.

My week went like this: I attended classes at La Salle, finishing around 4 P.M. I dashed to the nearby supermarket and was behind the meat counter by 4:30. I had a half-hour break for dinner, then went back to the huge refrigerator or meat counter until 9 or 10 P.M., depending on what day it was. Saturdays I worked from 8 A.M. till 11 P.M., with half-hour dinner breaks. Holiday seasons meant busy working days at the meat department: turkeys at Christmas and Thanksgiving, hams at Easter. Sundays I soaked my sore feet while studying and smiling, thinking of my growing bank account. It was the perfect job for a student and the highest pay in the supermarket, thanks to my eventual membership in the Amalgamated Meat Cutters of America. I still have my membership card. The Penn Fruit Company later went bankrupt and the union eventually became powerless.

Between work shifts, I studied and studied. Looking back, I realize that only the young and strong can keep up a schedule like that. But this particular job gave me an advantage over my future fellow students since meat cutting provided an advance look at my upcoming anatomy classes.

At one point, I almost lost my job. Saturday nights, about a half-hour before closing time, prices were reduced on perishables such as ground meat that could deteriorate over the Sunday closing. If the first reduction didn't sell it out, another reduction was made. Looking over my counter at the mothers and grandmothers waiting for the price reductions touched my heart. It seemed that they were always accompanied by small, poorly clad, hungry-looking children. I gave them "Over-

weight." If they asked for a half-pound, I gave them a pound
at the half-pound charge. As you can imagine, I acquired a
following. They would queue up at my station. This attracted
the attention of the watchful meat department manager.
"Scanlon, see me after you punch out on your time card." His
lecture was short. "We work on a small profit margin. Penn
Fruit is not a charitable institution. It's obvious what you are
doing, and you're fired."

I was shocked. The job was a necessity. I pleaded to his
cold face, "I'll have to leave school. Give me one more
chance, and it won't happen again."

His thoughts were almost readable, and I prayed. He knew
I was a good, hard worker and kept his payroll down. "Okay.
Your last chance. But I'll be watching you."

Another lesson: Don't give away another person's money,
no matter how worthy the cause.

By the following fall I had saved enough to start vet school.
My admission had been approved, and I was just in time. The
graduating class of 1946, my class, was the last one allowed
to start with only two years of college. The requirements were
changed to four years of college.

I had enough money for tuition, but little more. If, however,
I planned to eat, buy textbooks, sleep under a roof, and wear
clothing, I had to earn some money. Once again, I struck it
lucky. I got a job as a waiter and dishwasher at a sorority
house. It was a great job because it provided meals as well as
a small salary. The girls all ate like birds, and the waiters
were allowed to take "leftovers" back to our quarters. The
black lady cook, Melissa, was unimpressed by the chattering
and giggling "rich girls," as she called them, and gave "her
boys" the best steaks, chops, and cuts of roast. Melissa re-
sembled Scarlett O'Hara's Mammy in *Gone with the Wind*,
only she never faulted us. She was a sweetheart, always happy
and humming. You had to feel cheerful around her.

The job had other obvious attractions, but my classes and
studying left little time to socialize with the attractive "sis-

ters." It was frustrating, but my schedule demanded at least four hours' study each night. That was okay; I wouldn't have had enough money for dates anyway. It wasn't appropriate in those old days to ask a lady to pay her own way, though most of them had more money than I. My chances would have been slim anyway—the majority of them came from money, and preferred a "steady" from their own social class.

Renting a room with one or two other people was the cheapest way to live, so I shared a small third-floor room with Rufus Johnson, a Marylander. Rufe was good-looking, and while sloppy about our room, he was fastidious about his person and always dressed well. He was a born ladies' man. Except for his snoring and his disgustingly foul cigars, Rufus and I got along fine. The cigars were the major bone of contention. These weren't ordinary cigars, they were real stink bombs. They didn't come from anywhere local; he actually had them shipped to him—his only luxury. I put up a fuss about them, but Rufus won those arguments with stunning speeches proclaiming that it was his "constitutional and civil right" to smoke in his own room if he wanted to. Maybe his father was right; Rufe was in the wrong profession.

His father was a low-court judge who all but disowned Rufus when he discovered his son's intentions to become a "damn horse doctor." In his eyes, the law was the only noble profession and a lawyer's education the only one he would pay for. Rufus received a small living allowance through his mother, but nothing toward his tuition. Though the circumstances were different, we were in similar straits money-wise. My family would have given me the money if they'd had it; his had money but wouldn't give it. We both were in constant need of extra funds.

Rufus had a real way with ladies and was highly adept at buttering up the waitresses at the coffee shop across the street. We ate an awful lot of free doughnuts and drank purloined orange juice. Despite his success with the ladies, he thought he could better it, and he began raising a mustache.

"I think it will open the door to more mature pastures," was his rationale. I envied his zest for the chase, but I just wasn't in his league. Plus I had to put in two hours' study for his every one, which left me less time for pursuit.

Rufus was into money-making schemes. One day I walked into the room and saw him measuring the inside of our closet. When he heard me come in, he scrambled up and said, "I have a great idea for how we can make some extra money."

"How? Subletting the closet? Selling it to land developers?"

"No, seriously, Ed. I've been doing some reading, and I found out that prices for Dalmatian pups have gone up twenty percent in the last year. They're getting really popular with society types, and supply can't keep up with the demand."

"That's fine for anyone who has Dalmatian pups."

"That's it, that's it exactly!" he enthused. "We have to get some."

"But if they are so expensive," I reasoned, "how can we afford any?"

"Simple. We raise them ourselves. I know an Eastern Shore farmer who has a pregnant Dalmatian bitch and he'll sell her and the pups to us and take her back when they're weaned. We'll wean them and then sell them at top prices to your rich Main Liners. And, since the pups will have been raised by vet students, people can be assured they will be in the best of health."

I looked around our small room, wondering if Rufus saw the same room I did. I almost had to walk on my bed to get to my desk. There wasn't enough room for a small stuffed dog, let alone a bitch and a litter of pups.

"We'll use the closet as a whelping pen for the bitch. That's why I was measuring it. It looked big enough to me, but I figured I'd better check against what it says in the book. Don't worry, it's perfect." Apparently Rufus had been thinking this through carefully, but he didn't seem to be using the same logic that other people did.

"The pups won't be housebroken . . . we'll be cleaning day and night."

"We'll just put down lots of newspapers. I know a girl who works in the library who'll give us some—it'll be very sanitary." Rufus knew a girl everywhere, and they were all glad to help him out.

"It'll stink to high heaven!"

"Don't worry. As long as we change them often enough, it'll be fine. The landlady never comes here, and I already asked the guys downstairs. They don't give a damn."

"What about the money?" I asked. "I don't have any money to buy a brood bitch."

"Ed, you worry too much. We can just pay for her after the pups are sold."

"The farmer agreed to that?"

"Why wouldn't he? It's a sure thing."

Rufus gradually wore me down, mostly by repeating the profits he expected us to make. Compared to that, getting up early and missing an occasional lunch to take care of the pups didn't seem too much to ask.

"We'll take turns," he promised. "It'll only take a few minutes to walk the bitch and feed the pups. Really, there's no other way short of crime we can make this much money for almost no work."

Reluctantly, I agreed. I could use the money, and I was a little afraid that if I didn't join in the venture, I would come back to the room one day and find a dog in the closet anyway. Besides, wasn't this good practice for being a vet? "All right, all right. But you have to come back and walk her Saturday nights. I'm not missing any parties for this."

"We'll worry about that later. Right now, we have to call the farmer and find some lumber to close off the closet." Rufe believed in action.

As I suspected, there were flaws in the plan, but as time went by, we smoothed them out. We eventually cut out a lot of time and work that enabled us to turn over litters much faster.

We would buy whole litters just after they were weaned, thereby shortening the time we had them. We became a virtual puppy mill. We did make much-needed money, but the work was more than either of us expected. The noise was horrendous—again, good practice for later in my life. My wife always did credit Rufus and his scheme for the fact that I could sleep no matter how loudly our babies cried. How can one little baby compare to seven active, squealing Dalmatian pups two feet from one's ears?

But the smell was memorable. There was only one window and a small fan that did nothing but move the odors around. This was the inspiration for my hospital design, which demanded many, many windows with lots of cross-ventilation. The pine-scented deodorizer we used to cover the kennel smells was almost as bad as the smells themselves. The only thing that really seemed to help was Rufe's cheap cigars. "Smoke another one, Rufe," I'd beg. "Smoke another one, please!"

Our financial problems were soon to be over. We were deep into World War II, and the Army had taken over all the graduate schools at the University of Pennsylvania and other colleges and universities. We had entered the war, and the high command had decreed that to ensure a supply of physicians, dentists, and veterinarians, students would be drafted and activated as privates first class. We would then be assigned to the various schools—in other words, we would continue our educations at our present schools, but it would be at Uncle Sam's pleasure. Most of us were temporarily deferred and held a commission as inactive first lieutenants. We now had the option to resign our commissions, re-enlist as privates, and continue our schooling at Uncle's expense after a brief army basic training course. The other option offered was to be assigned to active field duty as officers. No one took that option.

We were put in uniforms, marched to mess, drills, and medical army lectures, and assigned to barracks. All our expenses were paid and we received a small monthly check. The

Army decided to speed up the supply of M.D.'s, D.D.S.'s, and V.M.D.'s; it therefore decreed no summer vacations, all holidays shortened, and extended daily hours with a full day's classes on Saturday. The result was that we would graduate in 1945 instead of 1946. The faculty members were upset. They had to shorten the content of some courses, and they had to put in longer days and hours. Initially their income was not increased, which added to their discontent. The bottom line was that we were the only class in the history of the veterinary school to complete the four-year course in three years. Consequently some of our training suffered, and we were pushed to limits we didn't know we could achieve. But there was a war on, and the Army was in command. When I read of the deaths of those in the battlefields, I felt lucky and guilty. Why me? Why was I so fortunate? All the students I knew felt guilt to some degree, but we rarely discussed it.

Vet school passed in a haze of army drills, classes, and the sheer overwhelming work of absorbing knowledge. As I look back, what I mostly see is a young man, puzzling over new material and concepts, reading, reading, reading. Fortunately, I have always enjoyed reading, but I don't remember much in the way of enjoyment then. While it all merges in my mind, I do have a few clear memories of those three years.

We all attended vet school with a constant fear of low grades. It was the fear of failure. We had that fear instilled in us the first day. I clearly remember the dean's admittance and "welcome" lecture in the auditorium. "Look around you," he said. "At least one in seven seats will be empty by graduation. Those will be the ones who failed." That greeting would be unheard of today.

One of the classes that caused mortality was the chemistry class conducted by the feared Dr. Jones, a brilliant chemist but perhaps an inadequate professor. We experienced our first student loss at his very first laboratory session. We entered the lab and were assigned lockers and seats alphabetically, which put a Mr. Schivelle from Tennessee next to me. While

waiting, we peered at the blackboards that surrounded three
sides of the room. They were all completely covered with mysterious, arcane formulas. I recognized a few elements, but felt
my stomach drop. I had studied chemistry in college, so I was
no newcomer, but this was profoundly beyond me. Mr. Schivelle and I exchanged a worried look.

Dr. Jones finally entered and welcomed us. Mr. Schivelle
raised his hand and asked in a thick but elegant Southern accent, "Dr. Jones, suh, what is all that gibberish on the blackboards?"

Sternly, Dr. Jones answered, "That 'gibberish,' young man,
is material you'll be tested on and be expected to know."

Schivelle slammed his locker door and announced, "I'm a
Princeton graduate and a chemistry major. That's all bullshit.
You're trying to intimidate us, not teach us." Exit Mr. Schivelle. One less to worry about. He couldn't have seriously
wanted to be a vet; no one would have given up that easily had
he been serious.

One of our two female students stands out in my mind for
an unexpected reason. She was very interesting because she
had no intention of practicing for a living after graduation.
Barbara Smythe came from South Africa, where her wealthy
family had huge holdings in livestock. She wanted to learn
about disease, prevention, and treatment so that she could
tend the family's animals. But it turned out that she never
went back to her troubled homeland. She fell in love with a
sophomore student and was married in our junior year. They
later practiced together. At our fiftieth class reunion, our
lovely Barbara was there, still married to the same man, still
glad of the decisions she had made as a youth.

Our other woman student transferred to law school after
two weeks of anatomy classes. Dissecting the dead flesh of animals and the stink of formaldehyde were too much. We lost
three more classmates the first year, one to tuberculosis.
Classes all day, long nights of study, plus the typical poor student nutrition often equaled illness. Back then tuberculosis

was still a constant specter, not an almost unheard-of disease. Two others succumbed to Dr. Jones's poisoning chemistry. We didn't lose anyone our second year, but in our third year one of the students in the class before us committed suicide by jumping off the lab building roof. It saddened us daily as we passed the spot.

Suddenly it was all over. Graduation was at hand. The many long years of study, work, and worry seemed like a dream. Sir Alexander Fleming, the recent discoverer of penicillin, spoke at our graduation. I don't recall his words, but that day I walked away with the paper I had been seeking for years. That was all I could think of, the diploma that said I was now Edward J. Scanlon, V.M.D., a graduate veterinarian at last. The long pursuit was finished, my goal achieved! My life as a vet could begin.

Occasionally I think back on my classmates and wonder. Did they find their careers as satisfying as I did mine? After spending all that time together, we suddenly scattered all over the country. Now and then we would run into each other at conventions and play the "whatever happened to . . ." game.

Rufe Johnson returned to the Eastern Shore of Maryland, his home. I surmised that his family forgave him when he became a successful vet and businessman. At one point, he modestly told me he was "interested in the racetrack there and in the chicken business," which translated that he owned a piece of each.

Our reunions, sponsored by the university every fifth year, have been ill attended. At our fiftieth in 1995, there were only four of us. Maybe everyone was so glad to leave they didn't want to return. Maybe they were just too busy. Maybe, like my old buddy Rufe, they had gone to their final rewards.

I can only hope they found their careers as satisfying and fascinating as I did.

three

At the Feet of the Master

My interview with the Great One was scheduled for 10:15 P.M. on a rainy Saturday night. The time seemed a little unusual, and it should have been a warning that time (especially my time) was of little interest to my hoped-for boss. I was so anxious to be hired as his intern that I would have appeared at 1:15 A.M. if requested—or should I say commanded. Otto Stader seldom requested!

The openings of the so-called interns were relatively few, as the job had to be close enough to the vet school to commute. Such associations with an experienced and practicing vet were hotly sought after by members of our senior class. The school provided the finest basic theoretical training but was necessarily short of hands-on practical training, so internship was the key to a working advantage.

The interns were provided a room or rooms over the participating hospital. Their duties varied, but essentially they administered evening and late-night treatments, as well as early-morning medications, to the hospitalized pets. On occasion they assisted with emergency surgery or emergency treatments. The interns also answered the after-hours emergency cases, presented at the hospital door, and evaluated and screened emergency phone calls. While not licensed or graduated, the interns were charged with giving first aid or emergency care until the vet on duty arrived to take over. These duties often resulted in severe sleep deprivation but were invaluable practical experience.

The internship I was seeking met the criterion of being close to school, about a half-hour's commuting time via public transportation. Most important of all, it was with the master of Ardmore Animal Hospital, a super-new facility owned and operated by Dr. Otto Stader, one of the most well-known and well-regarded veterinarians of the time. Dr. Stader was the recipient of many local, state, and national awards. He had been given the prestigious honor of the International Veterinary Congress award, Veterinarian of the Year. He was a pioneer in bone pinning for the correction of fractures and held patents on something called the Stader Splint.

Essentially, the Stader Splint was an ingenious method of correcting broken bones by allowing the operator to align and fix, as well as immobilize, the fractures through the use of steel pins and bars. It was especially useful in fractures that were difficult to cast. Simply put, by a clever use of pins inside the bone and plates outside the body, bones could be joined without damaging muscle or other tissue as much as usual. The Stader Splint was sold under license by General Electric Company on a royalty basis and was very useful in joining mandibular fractures in humans. Dr. Stader assisted in and directed its use in a number of human hospitals as well as in animal applications.

I arrived for my interview soggy from the rain, but five minutes early. Dr. Stader had a reputation for severity, and his physical appearance supported that. He was in his early fifties, clean-shaven, with crew-cut hair gray at the temples and slightly protruding gray-blue eyes, tall with a slender, whip-like build. His movements, while not actually jerky, gave that impression. His voice was not loud but clear and dominant, with terse, clipped words. He could have been brought in by central casting to play the Prussian General to perfection.

To my great initial pleasure, the Great One hired me as his intern. I admit I was surprised, because he gave no clue during the interview whether I was of interest or not. I was anxious, and his questions were few. He was very difficult to read, and I received no insights into his personality. His questions revolved mostly around my interest in orthopedics and surgery. Naturally, these were subjects that interested me, and I emphasized this interest.

He asked about my grades, which were average. He didn't seem to be bothered by that. "That's okay. In my experience the best vets come from the middle ground. The big brains don't always equate with practical work." This was a bit of a comfort, because I knew he was also interviewing a classmate who was considered very sharp and was in the top rank scholastically. I always had to work very hard for those elusive As.

Because the country was deeply engaged in World War II and I was finishing school at the "pleasure of the armed services" as a private first class, I had to receive permission from my superior officer to live outside the barracks. Dr. Stader arranged this by a single phone call to Brigadier General Kelser, dean of the school.

Our arrangement was that I was to live over the hospital, tend to medications in the early morning and evening, take in emergencies till the vet on call arrived, assist in emergency treatment, and answer the phone. I was free every Thursday afternoon and evening for personal needs, like laundry, medical or dental care, or an evening of socializing. Weekends, I was on duty. Every fourth Sunday I was free. Of course, my studies and homework were to be done in my spare time after

8 P.M., when the hospital hours were over. As far as payment went, after commuting expenses, I had about seven dollars a week plus a meal allowance. I did, however, have a refrigerator and hot plate, so I could save some money on food.

After my first week at Ardmore Animal Hospital, I was looking forward to my Thursday time off, but when I glanced at my work sheet I saw Dr. Stader had scheduled me for medications and a dislocated hip surgical reconstruction at 8:30 P.M.—after the hospital closed. I was to assist with the surgery. Dr. Stader made it clear that this was a privilege. The surgery was a new, novel approach, and I was both interested and fascinated enough to forfeit my time off willingly. I could catch up on my laundry next Thursday.

The usual treatment for a dislocated hip at that time was to force the ball-like end of the femur back into the socket-like portion of the pelvis and bandage the leg up under the abdomen to immobilize it. The animal would then hop on three legs during the healing time. This method was not always effective and certainly was uncomfortable for the patient. (The surgical reductions and "false" prosthetic hip replacements available today were not even visualized in the early '40s.) The new approach developed by the Great One involved three bone pins secured together by external metal pins in a triangular shape. He modestly called it the Stader Triangular Pin Reduction for dislocated hips.

At the end of the operation, Dr. Stader picked up the entire hind end of the pet's body by the attached triangular apparatus, raising it several inches off the table. This was a dramatic demonstration of the strength of the reduction. During healing, the animal could walk and stand almost normally, a great asset to a completely normal recovery. I really did feel I was associated with greatness. Even at Penn, very little bone pinning was being taught, and here I was privy to learn and participate in a new surgical advance.

Another such operation was scheduled for the next Thursday evening (naturally), as Dr. Stader was slated to demonstrate his new approach and technique before the annual convention of the American Animal Hospital Association in Chicago two weeks later. Despite the fact that I had dirty laundry accumulating and sundry small errands to do on my Thursday "off day," I felt I had best attend. Again, my schedule for medications, bandage changing, instrument sterilization, and surgical gown and drape preparation was to be done as though the off day were nonexistent, which I guess it was.

Dr. Frank Hankin, a very bright and progressive young veterinarian hailing from Denver, Colorado, was Dr. Stader's full-time associate. Actually, I had most of my contact with him, as Dr. Stader was frequently out of town, speaking at meetings and giving splint demonstrations. Dr. Stader, in effect, spoke most often through Dr. Hankin, who ran the hospital in his absence and to whom I directly reported.

It has been said that if one associates with a person closely and long enough, he or she assumes many of the associate's characteristics and thinking. Dr. Hankin proved this theory. Deliberately or unconsciously, he was a junior Dr. Stader. His speech, like that of his mentor, was sparse and direct. He had no sense of humor or perception of anything outside the task at hand. He and Dr. Stader would provide information as to the why and how of a certain procedure if questioned, but very little was volunteered. Apparently they thought learning was acquired through watchful silence.

They did give me minute instructions on the administration of medications and surgical after-care and on progress monitoring. I became an expert as well in the sanitation and maintenance of two operating and exam rooms and ensured the presence of sufficient sponges, tongue depressors, antiseptics, drugs, and all other necessary supplies. I was especially charged with having all surgical instruments sterile and in readiness. Words were not scarce when anything was out of place or in short supply.

So it was that having gone over two weeks without my Thursday off time, attending classes full time at school, studying at night, and with the occasional sleep interruption for an emergency, I became desperate enough to gather the courage to approach Dr. Hankin after the second hip surgery. I explained that I had things that I had to do and had put off because of missing my off days. I asked if I could have the coming Saturday off.

"You want this Saturday off? Is that what you're saying?"

Gulp. "Yes."

"Well, that's very irregular. I'll have to talk to Dr. Stader." This was reluctantly volunteered with a thoughtful frown. I felt like a supplicant, begging for my life.

He followed Dr. Stader into his private office. I was sure the Commander was having a "nip." It was well known that a bottle of Jack Daniel's occupied his upper right-hand desk drawer, along with a stack of breath fresheners.

Dr. Hankin returned a few minutes later. "Well, Dr. Stader agreed." I sighed with thanks. "But he told me to remind you that constantly thinking about time off is not good preparation for a successful career in veterinary medicine." I felt that this admonition about thinking of time off could actually have come from either of them. "You can thank me," he continued, "because Mrs. Hankin and I were planning on dining out and I'll have to cover for you." They had managed to make me feel guilty, and I didn't know why.

Drs. Hankin and Stader were to attend and demonstrate the Stader Triangular Pin Reduction at the national convention in Chicago, and to this end they had made arrangements for a replacement for Dr. Hankin. "Now, Dr. Rodgers is a good man. Maybe a little strict and bossy, but you can learn from him. He is very good with ear surgery for drainage of chronic ear canal infections," Dr. Hankin told me. Someone whom Dr. Stader and his shadow Dr. Hankin called "strict and bossy" was cause for some apprehension, but it would be for only three days.

A day before their scheduled departure, word arrived that Dr. Rodgers was suddenly ill and could not fulfill his commitments. The doctors called around frantically but no one of sufficient experience could be found on such short notice. Drs. Stader and Hankin conferred and eventually sent for me. They explained the situation and decided that I would replace Dr. Hankin and accompany the Great One as an assistant. Instead of being elated at the prospect of a trip to Chicago (the farthest away I had been at that time was Atlantic City) and happy with their confidence in me, I was taken aback and chiefly felt incompetent and apprehensive. "But surely," I objected, "you can pick up an experienced colleague in Chicago."

I didn't understand the politics. Dr. Stader explained, "The proceedings will be described and published in the annual report and in veterinary magazines and journals. Such a colleague's name would appear and diminish our credit. It might even seem as though he had had a part in the development." Dr. Stader could be winning when it suited him. "After all, it's ours. You know the procedure. No problem. You can handle it."

"But what about school? I can't get three days off." Plus there was the Army to deal with. I still was not convinced of my capability, although I was beginning to become intrigued. After all, I would meet and have the chance to hear some of the most prominent veterinarians in the country present papers and demonstrations.

With another smile, Stader said, "No problem. I can arrange it through the dean. You'll learn more at the convention than at school." Since we were not having exams, and knowing his connections, it was a done deal.

Dr. Hankin spoke. "You're lucky to have this opportunity and all expenses paid in the bargain." I knew he was keenly disappointed. He too put in long, hard hours and was not highly paid. Associates of the Great One never were. Many vets sought his association, so he could call the tunes.

When I had been present at the two previous operations, I had only anesthetized the dog, shaved and prepped the surgical area, and had the drapes, gowns, gloves, and instruments laid out. And of course, cleaned everything up afterward. Dr. Hankin had hooked up the intravenous fluid and monitored the state of anesthesia through the surgery, injecting more if necessary. He had handed all instruments to the surgeon instantly on cue as needed. As assistant, I would be responsible for all those duties, plus my own. I had visions of being unable to locate the proper instruments under Stader's glare or the patient starting to come out of anesthesia through my failure to monitor. This in front of hundreds of vets, peering at me in the brilliant lights of the amphitheater.

"Good, Dr. Scanlon, it's settled then." He was always formal and professional and although I had not earned the title yet, I was always Dr. Scanlon and he Dr. Stader. First names were unthinkable with him or Dr. Hankin.

During the week prior to our trip, I alternated pleasant anticipation with the fear of some sort of mistake or failure. I was vain enough to have leaked my upcoming plum to several classmates. I couldn't resist using my bragging rights.

Three days before our departure, an odd thing happened.

"Dr. Scanlon, here's ten dollars. Take my car, go to the junkyard on Fremont Street, and buy the best used john you can." These rapid, terse directions made no sense at all.

"John? Dr. Stader, I don't understand."

He looked at me. "You know, a crapper, a john, a used toilet." And he slammed the door as he left.

Like a well-trained robot, I performed. The questions I wanted to ask, I choked down. A john? Why would he want a john, especially a used one? All the hospital johns were in good working order.

No way could I know that I was instrumental in the first step in the development of the product later sold as the Toilet Alert. The genesis of the Alert was constipation, insomnia, and Dr. Stader's aversion to a plumber's bill. Of course, I pieced all this together much later and from various sources.

It seemed he spent considerable time on the john due to a sluggish bowel and frequently during insomnia bouts. Which came first was unclear. While on the "throne," he was irritated by a leaking or dripping toilet. The quiet of the house at night accentuated the drip, drip, drip. Dr. Stader called a plumber to correct it. He presented what Dr. Stader considered an outrageous bill, and to add insult to injury, the drip recurred.

Dr. Stader decided to investigate the problem personally. I never had the time or the interest to understand the problem or its correction, but I did see the final Alert packaged in several sample parcels in his private office. Dr. Stader selected a semi-transparent package with red printing advising that the Alert was "guaranteed to correct a leaky toilet." It looked to me like a white plastic sleeve. I didn't have the nerve to open it and examine the contents, much less to question him. He volunteered no information and apparently the tool's development and sales were not that interesting to him. It was supposedly to be sold in many hardware stores, was geared to the amateur plumber, and would make considerable money—according to hospital gossip.

Mrs. Walsh, who was Dr. Stader's secretary and receptionist at that time, was enthused and vocal about the Alert's merits and potential earnings. "The genius has struck again," she announced. "Just think of all the money those poor people will save on plumber's bills."

"He's never talked much about it to me," I mused.

She smiled. "Well, he's naturally modest and doesn't consider it important. I think he feels it's beneath his professional status to be involved with plumbing."

That about summed it up, to my thinking. I never met a person less interested in money. To Dr. Stader, it was simply a bothersome fact of life. On occasion, he would wire Mrs. Walsh for money because he had gone off on a trip without any. Mrs. Walsh once confided, "Thank heavens he has me. He doesn't even know how much his royalty checks are or what's in the bank account." To my surprise, she added, "The royalty income from the splint is not as big as everyone thinks.

General Electric takes a portion out of his end for those big full-page advertisement costs." She was pretty smart. "The market is not really that large and he has no control over their marketing costs. You see, those ads also advertise G.E., so they don't care." My respect for Mrs. Walsh, whom I had mostly considered a little vapid and vain, went up enormously. I was just beginning to know her and had yet to learn her many abilities.

I was somewhat bewildered as well as surprised at this information about Stader's finances. Like many people, I assumed he was very well off from his royalties. I knew the hospital costs were unusually high. Dr. Stader was chairman of the Committee on Hospital Construction for the American Animal Hospital Association and had published several articles on ideal construction. Everything was the best and the most costly—stainless steel, ceramic tile, the newest and best in construction. Plus it was built on a very costly piece of commercial land. I pondered some elementary business facts. If his hospital had been built largely with mortgage funds, his debt service would be huge and out of line for the practice's gross income. Wow! The Great One had money problems! The thought was hard to digest. I voiced such to Mrs. Walsh.

"Yes, if his royalties from the new distemper vaccine [another Stader product in the works] or the Alert don't pan out, he'll need another mortgage." A direct, serious look from Mrs. Walsh at that point. "You're in the family and I know you'll keep this to yourself." I nodded, completely amazed.

My hero, the genius, the pioneer, with money problems, just like me. It was hard to comprehend.

If he had financial problems, he was unaware of them or just ignored them. Mrs. Walsh had our first-class airline tickets ready, plus a fine suite reserved at the Drake Hotel in Chicago, the convention site. My excitement was growing, although my confidence in my ability had not kept pace. I could still visualize my dropping the pin chuck, the handle in which the pins were inserted for screwing into the bone. I decided to bring an extra one.

We arrived and were ensconced in our opulent suite by 4:30 P.M. We were scheduled to perform the demonstration at 8 A.M., the first on the next day's program, which ran from 8 A.M. to 4 P.M., with a short luncheon break. This allowed, I found out, for a customary long, social hour and a half before the dinner.

Dr. Stader directed me to locate via page boy a Dr. Franklin, who was in charge of the entire convention. "Identify yourself and he'll show you where to set up, or he'll turn you over to someone. They will supply our patient. The amphitheater will be available since today's meetings are over. Look me up in the bar if there's a problem. Eat whatever you like and charge it to our suite."

I questioned, "A page boy? What's that?" I had a general idea of what a page boy was, but I had never used or even seen one. This was my first overnight stay in a large hotel.

"Go to the registration desk, Dr. Scanlon. They'll take care of it."

Everything went smoothly, and thus was born my lifelong reliance on "front desk" people and concierges when I had the opportunity to travel later in life. I found they could solve almost any problem you could think up, and their solutions were often highly creative.

I had our surgical packs, drapes, gloves, and gowns set up along with our instruments in the same location they would have been in our own surgery. Of course, the dog provided for the demonstration had no hip luxation, and I would remove the pins after the demonstration while he was still under anesthesia. (It would have been unkind to have a dog with that painful an injury just waiting around until the convention was held. It was deemed more merciful to "fake" the surgery.)

Our dog was a nondescript, medium-sized brown mix breed (an all-American, for sure), with a very friendly tail and floppy, hound-like ears. Somewhere I had read that if dogs were allowed to breed naturally and not selectively, the canine species would eventually come to resemble our patient, more or less. At that time, the American Kennel Club recognized over one hundred breeds, and this guy wasn't one of them by any stretch.

I've always had a habit of talking to my patients and believe they respond by tail, head, and facial expression. "Brownie," I assured him, "you'll thankfully never know what you're facing and will feel only mild discomfort after I remove the pins. I'll see you get some pain control pills for a couple days just in case. What we're going to do tomorrow will help so many of your brothers and sisters that it will be worth it." He obviously agreed, and showed his approval with a few thumps of his tail on the paper-covered floor of his pen. Fortunately he had no fear of the future. Being a dog has some advantages.

I checked him over and found a prominent vein for the anesthesia needle and the IV. Thankfully I returned him to his portable cage and hung a "No Food or Water" sign as a precaution. Then I sat on top of his cage, looked at Brownie, and mentally ran through the whole procedure in detail for the umpteenth time. By this time, I had developed a reasonable degree of confidence but thought of Murphy's Law: "Anything that can go wrong, will." I tried, but I could not conjure up anything that could go amiss. That innocent confidence shows how young I was back in those days.

It was approaching dinnertime, and I was about to enter the huge dining room when I heard a page boy calling for Dr. Edward Scanlon. He directed me to the bar. "A Dr. Otto Stader is looking for you."

Dr. Stader was at the bar with a large person whom I recognized. Dr. Lacroix was often a convention speaker and his photograph was occasionally in the vet journals. He had devised an operation known, appropriately enough, as the Lacroix Ear Drainage. It was for chronic ear infections that are now treated with a course of antibiotics. (If I were asked to list the most far-reaching changes during the twentieth century—most of which I've seen—I would put antibiotics in the top three.)

Stader briefly introduced me as his intern and then drew me aside. "Everything okay?"

"Yes," I assured him, "fine. I checked and re-checked."

My orders came swiftly. "Be in the amphitheater by 7:30 and anesthetize the dog. Have him prepped and draped with the IV hooked up by 7:50. When I come in at 8, I will briefly describe the condition and the corrective procedure over the loudspeaker and then proceed with the surgery."

He reached to the bar and downed the last of a dark liquid—Jack Daniel's, no doubt. "Now don't worry. Everything will be fine. When the surgery is completed, I'll lift up the hind end to demonstrate the strength of the apparatus. You douse the operating light, unscrew and remove the assembly, disconnect the IV, and meanwhile I'll be taking audience questions." I noted his slightly flushed face as he looked to the barman for a refill. It seemed to me a little early for such a vigorous "happy hour."

Dr. Stader admitted to me that he was looking forward to meeting a lot of his old buddies from around the country at the bar after dinner. He always seemed such a loner and so indifferent to companionship and camaraderie that this sign of friendliness surprised me. Well, I thought, I had enough to worry about and after all, he was a veteran of many seminars and conventions. "I left a call for 6:30 A.M.," he said and dismissed me by turning his back.

Being on Dr. Stader's expense account (another entirely new experience for me, and one I sensed I could grow to enjoy), I ordered the finest: a lobster/filet combination, all four courses, and a rich chocolate cake dessert. I savored every delightful bite of the gargantuan meal. With Dr. Stader's disregard for money, he either wouldn't notice or wouldn't care. Mrs. Walsh might be a different story, as she microscopically examined every bill and checked all the math. I came to treasure this habit when she came to work for me, but at this time it gave me a faint twinge of guilt. As I was technically in the army, my breakfasts and lunches on campus were paid for by Uncle Sam, but I had to skip many dinners to perform my intern duties. It had been an austere time in my life, and this luxury, even if for one meal, was sublime. Somewhat stuffed and at peace, I signed a generous tip over our room number. The haughty waiter didn't consider the tip as generous as I did, or perhaps I didn't look like the type who could tip like that, because he insisted on seeing my room key.

I spent the evening in the ornate, elegant lobby, pretending to read a newspaper but really eyeing the prosperous passers-by. I recognized several prominent veterinarians from their pictures in the professional journals, of which all senior students were avid readers. I remember feeling special that night, as if I were allowed a glimpse of a world to which I didn't quite belong—yet. I felt all things were possible, and I hoped I would attend many of these conventions. I even had a fore-shadowing of occasions when I would be an honored speaker.

I have never needed a sleeping pill, never suffered insomnia as did the Great One, so when I stretched out in the over-sized bed, it was but a few minutes till I was asleep. I was awakened suddenly by the crash of a bureau falling. I flipped on the bedside light. The clock had to be wrong—it read 3:20 A.M.

Dr. Stader stared at the tipped-over bureau with a how-dare-you glare (I had seen that one before). "Are you okay?" I asked.

He turned the glare to me. "Of course," he intoned as he staggered to the bed on the other side of the nightstand. "Turn off that darn light," came a muffled voice from the fully clothed, prone body.

I complied, but sleep didn't come back quickly. My God, after coming all this distance, the expense, the preparation, the disgrace if Dr. Stader couldn't make the presentation. Having had some personal experience with hangovers, and having observed my fellow students' ill effects, I knew they often lasted till noon of the next day, and that was when our revels had ended by 1 A.M. I was truly worried; our morning call was barely three hours away. The deep snores from my roommate and the sound of the bureau falling rang in my ears while the staggering gait and collapse of the Great One passed before my eyes. I took these as sure signs of a no-show, or at least a botched demonstration. Murphy's Law had struck in a way I hadn't considered, and I was near hyperventilation.

I tried to mentally prepare a speech for my call to Dr. Franklin. How could I minimize the damage? "Dr. Stader has a bad virus and is sick. You'd best not count on our presentation." No, that wouldn't work. Undoubtedly he had had company in the bar. A virus wouldn't sell. Maybe food poisoning? No. I had better just say he was ill and not commit to a cause. I would call the house M.D. Surely my new friends at the front desk could help me. They probably had a substitute program for such a situation.

I dozed fitfully. I was awakened, very shortly it seemed, by the alarm and telephone sounding off simultaneously. As I turned to shut off the alarm, I heard a voice. "Yes, this is room 812. Thank you for such a prompt and correct wake-up call." There stood the former drunk, showered, clean, hair still wet but combed. And cheerful to boot!

I saw the rare Stader smile. "This is your big day, Doctor. Rise and shine." Clearly I was in a league that I neither understood nor belonged in. A few short hours ago I was sure the Commander was down and out; now he was apparently as fresh as the proverbial daisy and exuding more energy than I had. I felt washed out, exhausted, and the day had yet to begin.

The demonstration of the Stader Triangular Pin Reduction for dislocated hips went off as smoothly as I could have dreamed. The surgeon's eyes may have been bright pink where the sclera should have been white, and I might have had to sponge his sweating forehead more often than usual, but overall it was near perfect. The moment when he lifted Brownie by the steel bar was filled with as much drama and audience appreciation as Dr. Stader could have wanted. He concluded by thanking his audience and (would you believe?) his "excellent assistant."

Brownie was everything I had hoped for. His vein was prominent and my IV needle true. He was a young, strong, healthy dog and responded exactly as wished for, requiring a minimum of anesthesia. I did my best to keep my promise to him regarding postoperative pain suppression. Dr. Franklin assured me the medication would be given for a couple of days. "Then what?" I asked. "What happens to him next?"

Dr. Franklin looked at me in a strange way. "The same thing that happens to them all. They go back to the pound, get adopted or euthanized."

This was the real world. Brownie was a pawn in the veterinary educational process. He served as a vehicle to demonstrate a new, better procedure. His thanks was a possible but unlikely adoption or euthanasia after a so-called holding period. Adoption was unlikely, as most grown dogs were not as desirable as the cuddly, lovable pups. This was very depressing to me. I had chosen this profession, but no way did it seem fair as I looked at Brownie. He returned my look and my ear massage with a happy expression and tail thumps.

I left with a heavy heart and continued depression. I was powerless against the situation. His fate was out of my hands. I knew what in all probability would be his thankless reward. This experience saddened me, and I felt the burden of the dreadful fate of countless animals like him. Along with the sadness there came a feeling of resentment at a system that rewarded our soldiers in the war against disease and pain in such a way.

Mentally wrestling with this new disenchantment with my beloved profession, I tried to justify Brownie's fate. Thousands of humans, including innocent children, died slow, painful deaths from preventable starvation. At least euthanasia was painless. It didn't work. I still felt terrible. I could mentally see and feel his trusting, dark eyes on me.

However, I did come away from this unnerving and painful

part of my trip with some positive feelings. I firmly resolved to do my utmost to see that the Brownies of the world were given the best possible treatment, affection, and care. I also planned to seek and explore other possible options. Surely the profession could find a better answer.

Upon my return to the usual routine at Ardmore Animal Hospital, I perceived a change in my relationship with the Commander. No word of thanks after being roused from sleep for an emergency or for extra hours, but rather I had a feeling of being more accepted, more respected. He volunteered more information on medical and surgical procedures and problems. This was rewarding, as my previous status had been more that of a lackey. I now felt more of an equal, an associate, instead of just the hired hand.

Dr. Stader even confided in me about his problem with squirrels. It seemed the bird feeders in his treasured garden were constantly being raided by his enemy: crazed and avaricious squirrels. "Now, the solution is simple," he said. "I know just how to get them." He had applied his ingenious mind to it. "I have worked it out by body weight. When the heavy squirrel hits the feeder, I have a battery-operated shock that knocks him off. The birds are so much lighter that they won't set off the shock." He was convinced that this would be a big seller. Mrs. Walsh and I had trouble making him understand that this wouldn't be greeted with universal joy. Not everyone, we explained, disliked squirrels as fiercely as he did. Some people thought the "flying rats" were cute and enjoyable.

The man had unlimited endurance and was energized by problems. He would tackle the largest puzzles in our profession, yet nothing was too small to interest him and challenge him to find a solution.

I learned that prior to turning exclusively to small-animal medicine and surgery, he was renowned in his farm practice as a specialist on bovine pregnancy and fertility. He was a pioneer in fluid therapy. I was in awe of and devoted to his proficiency, knowledge, and achievements. But he was lacking as a human being. His temperament was cold, aloof, and remote to all his associates, but especially to his kennel men, who were the lowest on the animal hospital totem pole. To me, they were important both as contributors to the pets' care and as co-workers and human beings.

Most kennel men of those years were uneducated, had little ambition, and had problems with alcohol. After all, their duties consisted of cleaning cages and pens and taking animals on exercise runs. Feeding and watering their charges, exercising them at outdoor runs (which were roofed for inclement weather), and returning them several times a day rounded out their duties. And yet, the vets depended on the kennel men to report on the pets' appetites, bowels, and general attitudes. Several of the best kennel men I had over the years were slightly mentally handicapped. They were devoted to their work, loved the patients, and took great pleasure in the love the pets showed them. They were mostly conscientious, and it seemed they felt they had a home in the hospital where they were appreciated and important.

I have had kennel people cry with sorrow on the occasions when a patient died or had to be "put down." One of my handicapped kennel men would refuse to bring a patient to the table to be euthanized. Despite my efforts to explain that we had lost the battle and the only merciful and loving thing left was to end the misery, he just couldn't face it. I understood because, despite knowing it was a release from suffering, despite knowing there was no chance for life of any quality, it was always difficult and unpleasant for me. I am sure my colleagues felt the same way, although it was a topic we rarely discussed.

During the later years of my practice, the kennel "man" changed sexes. It became the almost exclusive domain of women, who simply did the job better. They seemed to focus on the "caring" aspect of the job and to realize that, although the clean-up was critical, they could make a major contribution to the animals' healing and welfare with their compassion. They didn't consider the work menial, and the animals seemed to "come around" faster.

Dr. Stader and Dr. Hankin had a constantly changing roster of kennel men. This forced me into assuming more work, as the new people required more "checking up on" to see that the pets that were boarding, as well as the patients, were not neglected. It was especially important to keep an eye on the water bowls, seeing that they were full and clean. Although the bowls were heavy, there was always a dog who could overturn them.

Overall, my "internship" with Dr. Stader and my many miscellaneous duties gave me an exposure to the practical side of small-animal medicine that I just couldn't get in vet school alone. At the time, and even more so in retrospect, I considered it invaluable. It gave me some confidence and experience, but most of all, it saved me from a lot of future mistakes.

The Great One really surprised me when the end of my time with him arrived. I could hardly ever recall him saying "thanks" or "well done" at any time in our entire association. I sometimes wondered if the lack of appreciation was due to any lack on my part. On the occasions when he roused me from sleep to help him with an emergency surgery, he would, at its conclusion, just strip off his gloves, mask, and green gown and walk away. Not even a civil good-night.

My small bag was packed. I was ready to walk out for the last time, to leave Ardmore Animal Hospital. Mrs. Walsh had informed me that the Commander wanted to see me briefly before I left. I assumed he wanted to say good-bye and, if he was in an unusually good mood, offer good luck as well.

"Dr. Scanlon, come in, sit down." He waved me to the plush chair next to his desk as I appeared in the open door to the inner sanctum. He eyed me directly, and I had his rare full attention. He was momentarily silent as he took out what appeared to be a small checkbook. He was, I assumed, finishing some private business, as Mrs. Walsh made out all personnel and other business checks and I had already received my final paycheck.

He finished writing, detached a check, then swiveled in his chair and handed it to me. "Dr. Scanlon, here's a little something to show my appreciation of your work for me." *Appreciation,* I said to myself. *He does know the word, after all.* I glanced at the check and I was flabbergasted. It was drawn in the amount of $100, which was more than ten weeks' pay.

"Dr. Stader, this is most generous of you," I breathed.

I received a real Stader smile, as he said, "I don't think so, not for the best goddamned intern I ever had." I was almost overcome with emotion, not just for the check, which was an unexpected godsend, but by his obvious sincerity and his effort to say a genuine thank-you. It was difficult for him.

He rose, extended his hand, and said, "Well, you'll have your diploma soon. Remember, if I can ever help you in any way, just call me. I mean it." I knew he did, for he was a man who was always to the point, and always true to what he said.

I left him after our last meeting as I had after our first: confused. I had been with him perhaps three minutes at our parting, but I think of it frequently. He was a man of intense contradictions, strong intellect, terrible people skills, and massive ego and will. Was he completely out of character at our last meeting? Or couldn't he show his character? Or didn't I know him well enough to judge his character?

He had left his mark on the profession and on me, I thought as the hospital door closed. He had been awarded the International Veterinary Congress award, the highest on the planet, and at that moment I would have re-awarded it. His year-long coldness, aloofness, and arrogance were forgotten for the moment. He was again my vet hero.

four

First Job — at the SPCA

Several months before graduation, the great job scramble began. Most seniors were scurrying all over the country being interviewed by hoped-for employers. Very few had the financing or confidence to hang out their shingle. It was obvious by that winter that the Allies were winning the war, and my classmates and I had the incredible luck to be honorably discharged from the army almost simultaneously with graduation. I was on a winning streak, as my proposal of marriage was accepted. We were married the week after graduation. Boy, did I need a job.

I interviewed with a veterinarian in Pinehurst, North Carolina, who wanted a recent graduate to work in his practice, which included a new small-animal hospital. He was the only vet in the area and had a monopoly on the patients from the famous Pinehurst Winter Harness Horse Training Center. Horses had been a lifelong love of mine and I was very interested. I would assist with his equine patients and participate in the hospital's growth.

It seemed perfect for me, and I was about to sign a year's contract when practicality set in. My wife and I were not Southerners. She especially would have no friends in the then-small community of Pinehurst. Since we wanted to start our family immediately, she would be pregnant and away from family and familiar surroundings. It would be most difficult, because she would be alone most days and many evenings. So Pinehurst was written off, along with the thought of any equine practice.

Although I would have loved it, a racetrack equine practice association was out. Racetrack vets were always on the road—racetrack to racetrack, farm to farm. (At that time I couldn't know that my love of horses would be indulged and result in a lifelong interest and pleasure. I would be fortunate enough to own and race Standardbred harness horses for almost thirty-five years. As I write this, I still enjoy supervising and helping with the training of my horses, watching them run, and even occasionally winning.)

To have any family life, which was of primary importance to me, it became increasingly obvious that I should work in a small-animal practice. My hard but fruitful internship with Dr. Stader at Ardmore Animal Hospital had shown me that, despite the hours, I enjoyed it. I could be happy in that specialty, so I made up my mind that my goal would be to get experience, save money, and eventually open my own hospital.

Meanwhile, I found and was offered what seemed to be the ideal position with the Pennsylvania SPCA. It offered a wealth of clinical experience and the magnificent sum of $65 a week for three morning hours a day in their clinic. (I am not being sarcastic—$65 was a princely sum in those days—men raised families in an adequate standard of living on that amount of money in the 1940s!)

It would be perfect. We could live in our home area. I could, after a year or two, look forward to opening my own practice. I could make contacts, make house calls, build a following. The potential and future there seemed wonderful and boundless, just what the doctor ordered.

The SPCA's free clinic, which theoretically was for those unable to afford the services of a private vet, served sixty to eighty patients daily, six days a week. The staff consisted of a chief veterinarian, Dr. Kinemond, and his two assistants. In theory, as the third on-staff vet, I would see around twenty patients in the three-hour morning clinic, about seven an hour. It would be a great learning experience, and it would leave the rest of the day free for house calls. I signed a year's contract. After three months, if my work was satisfactory, I was promised a raise to $75 a week. (The raise was a myth. Vets were told at raise time that there was no money in the budget after all.)

What a mistake, and how naive I was. The chief and his other assistant, who each had a private practice, were frequent no-shows, or late. That meant I had to see their patients too, and there was no way I could provide adequate care for ten or twelve patients in an hour. I worked four, sometimes five and six hours at what had been promised to be a three-hour part-time job.

I was horrified at the "death wagons." The SPCA had a number of specially built trucks that answered emergency calls for accidents, dog fights, whatever. They also picked up strays. The wagons were equipped with a bypass so that the toxic exhaust fumes could be directed to a rear airtight chamber. There, animals deemed hopeless by the agent were euthanized by the diverted fumes. This was barbaric, not at all an easy death, but it was the accepted practice at the time.

I shudder to describe the death wagons' functions. Every day, twelve to twenty cats and dogs had to be put down. Strays and pets turned in for adoption were held for three days. If no homes were available, they were gassed in the death wagons. There was simply no room or funds to keep them longer. There would be an equal number of replacements the following day.

When I understood what was going on, I was disgusted and

charged into the president's office. "We are supposed to be the Society for the Prevention of Cruelty to Animals. Your euthanasia procedure is cruel. Have you seen those animals climbing the walls of the wagons, gasping for breath? If we don't change to lethal injection, I quit."

"Dr. Scanlon, that is a fine suggestion," replied the austere, bone-thin president, whom we will call Mr. Phillips. "You are now in charge of all euthanasia procedures." That meant he expected me to perform all euthanasias personally. It was a punishment that I was not prepared to take. I retaliated by training an assistant to proficiently perform the necessary but heartrending task. I couldn't possibly put all those animals to death, day in, day out.

I was, in effect, stuck. The prospect of getting another job was slim. I needed the money (daughter number one was on her way) and I had signed a contract. There was no choice but to live up to my obligation and make the best of the situation.

Dr. Kinemond resigned after several months and I was named chief veterinarian. I fired the other no-show vet and replaced him with a more willing colleague. There was no difficulty in finding a third vet. Things improved, but I was still unhappy with the position. In the clinic, with the pressure of time, I was often forced to make a snap diagnosis and prescribe treatment I wasn't comfortable with. It was unfair to my patients and I knew it. Most vets have a touchy conscience.

Taking advantage of my additional authority, I tried to upgrade the clinic. I demanded and received another lay assistant. She took all histories and symptoms from waiting owners, giving the vets more examination time. Supposedly, it was a free clinic for the financially distressed or poor pet owner. Many took advantage. I noticed fine cars, certainly better than I owned, in the parking lot. Many owners were expensively dressed and I frequently saw diamond rings with the stones turned palmward to hide them. Again, there was nothing I could do. We couldn't demand financial statements.

The donation box was usually filled with small coins at the end of clinic hours. I wrote a sign that read "Drugs are expensive. Help us." My assistant placed at least five one-dollar bills in a new Plexiglas container before hours. These measures almost quadrupled our donations, which was a hit with the front office. Still, my drug allowance was not increased a penny. I was forced to mix and continue dispensing many outdated remedies. This was especially galling, as during my internship with Dr. Stader, I had been able to see that my patients had the best, most up-to-date and effective care available. Whenever possible, I wrote prescriptions rather than hand out ineffective, but free, drugs. This proved unpopular with both clients and management. Arguing with Phillips was useless. The fact that more effective drugs were available meant nothing.

In the summer, pets' skin problems were numerous. Almost every third patient was afflicted. The cause was the increase in external parasites, compounded by ignorant or careless owners. Fleas were the major offenders, but ticks and lice also participated in the blood feast. I had a good idea and inaugurated a free Saturday-morning dip. It was similar to the old-fashioned cattle and sheep dips. Instead of the animal swimming through the dip, though, we carefully immersed it in a tub, first applying an ointment to protect the eyes. The results were popular, effective, and gratifying to all. Although not practicing the quality medicine I wished to, I was contributing to the welfare of animals. The novel dips even generated some newspaper coverage. Phillips liked that, and I was pleased to get some favorable publicity.

I was beginning to get requests for private house calls. This was permitted and considered to be a job perk. I welcomed them because, while our savings account was slowly growing, it wasn't growing quite as fast as my wife's tummy.

I remember one call vividly. "Dr. Scanlon, can you come soon? My two dogs have been in a fight and they are bitten badly." I carefully repeated and wrote down the address. This was routine, as the city was a maze of small streets and row houses. Despite my map and my habit of clarifying directions, it was easy to get lost. The house was on a corner, but the windows were boarded up. The number and street checked with my notes. Had I made a mistake? No. The door was opened on my first knock. I entered and looked around. Something was strange. Then light dawned. The walls of the adjoining row house had been removed and it was two houses in one.

Glancing at the several painted young ladies sitting around, more light dawned. I was in a house of "ill repute," a novel and unexpected experience. The woman who answered the door was the Miss Sullivan who had called, and from her take-charge attitude, I figured she was the madam.

"Dr. Scanlon, please follow me. The dogs are in the kitchen." One was a sizable black-and-tan Doberman, the other an enormous boxer. Each had a number of large but superficial skin wounds. Miss Sullivan said she had stopped the hemorrhaging with compression bandages. As I examined the dogs, I realized Miss Sullivan had not been entirely honest when she called. "These are not bite wounds, Miss Sullivan," I said, looking at her. "They are too clean; not at all like puncture wounds from teeth. They are knife or razor wounds, but fortunately they aren't deep."

"Yes," she admitted. "We had a problem with a drunken client last night. We tried to get rid of him by showing the dogs. He pulled a knife."

The dogs were not attack dogs. I could tell—they were too easy to handle. They were used as a deterrent to frighten someone. Given their large spiked collars and their size, they would probably be quite effective in most situations.

"Miss Sullivan," I advised, "I'd best take them to my colleague's hospital. There is a lot of cleaning, debriding, and suturing needed here. The wounds are probably already infected." There was a fellow starving local vet who gladly, for a fee, allowed me the use of his facility for my few surgeries.

52   She was the madam and the boss. "I want them treated

here. Otherwise I would have taken them to a hospital myself." She spoke not sharply, but forcefully. "I've had nursing
experience and"—smiling encouragement—"I know you can
handle it. We've heard of your work at the SPCA."

Flattery and money were hard to resist. "Okay. I'll be back
with the instruments and drugs in a half-hour." Saving face, I
added, "It would be easier and better at the hospital, though."

The repairs took several hours. The large kitchen table
was my operating table and Miss Sullivan was an able assistant. To inject some levity, I remarked, "You handle the instruments like you could do this job as well as a vet."

She looked at her gloved hands. "If I had the clippers, instruments, drugs, and sutures, maybe I could." She was serious, a note of pride. "I was a pretty good operating-room nurse
at one time."

My, my. From operating-room nurse to brothel madam?
There was a story here, and I was to gather it piecemeal on the
follow-up visits.

After completing the surgeries, I had to stay around for a
half-hour to be certain the dogs came out of the light general
anesthesia. Miss Sullivan brewed us some tea, which seemed
to fit her very slight Irish brogue. She practically and proudly
stated that she had the finest "house" in the city. "My girls are
the prettiest and get twice-monthly exams. Take your pick,
anything you want will be on the house." She airily waved her
hand in the direction of the parlor.

"Thank you, Miss Sullivan. I'm tempted, but I'm a happily
married man," I said nervously and probably somewhat prud-
ishly.

She laughed through even white teeth. "They are our best
customers, those happily married men." How naive I must
have seemed to her.

She insisted on paying me then and there. "Why don't we
wait," I suggested. "I'll have to make a few follow-up calls,
remove stitches, and give them more penicillin."

She was a shrewd businesswoman. "No. You'll charge me

more then. It'll give you too much time to think of all the work."

I laughed. "Suit yourself."

I then asked for what was, for me, quite a large fee. "That's fair." She looked at me as she slowly pulled up her skirt. Around her shapely thigh was a miniature money belt. She unsnapped it, counted out the exact amount, and added $50. "My girls earn that much on a Saturday night. Up your fees," she counseled.

Kathy, as she insisted I call her, was an interesting person, and I must admit I was curious, as she was certainly someone outside my ken. Physically, she was good-looking with very Irish coloring: copper hair, fair skin, blue eyes. She had excellent cheekbones. She was not the least bit brash or coarse, was probably around forty-five, and without being obvious, exuded sensuality. Kathy must have been stunning in her prime.

She had a cup of tea ready at the conclusion of my follow-up visits. She wasn't in a hurry, as there was little upstairs action in the afternoon, and I had few other calls, so we would chat. I felt she enjoyed my company. Maybe people who didn't want anything from her weren't that common in her daily life.

Her story was simple. She and her mother had been abandoned by her father. Her mother was an Irish immigrant who supported them as a live-in servant. This was where Kathy learned her manners—by watching her mother's employers. She attended nursing school. I never learned the details about how she actually switched professions, but she did say, "I learned there was far more money to be made in the bedroom than in the operating room." Kathy seemed extremely well-adjusted and made no apologies or excuses for what she did. This was certainly not the "fallen woman" I had heard about in my Catholic schooling.

She was a good source of new clients. She had many affluent city contacts who could afford and wanted house calls for their pets. Among them, she included (and sent to me) the

local Mafia boss to whom she had to pay "protection" and the
local police precinct captain, to whom she also had to make
payments. She frequently complained to me about the
"leeches," as she called them. She talked freely; I had become her friend as well as her vet. "Sure the house is profitable," she said, throwing up her hands. "The johns are waiting in line, but my God, the overhead."

She continued as a loyal client when I opened my hospital. She also remained a friend for many years, and in fact presented me with a $100 savings bond upon the birth of my first
daughter. She was down-to-earth, ladylike, and humorous. It
wasn't hard to understand how she was a success. Too bad she
hadn't chosen a legal business for her talents.

The SPCA provided another good source of income, and
that was the house calls for castrating male cats and dogs and
spaying females. I could never understand, with the huge
population of unwanted animals ending up on its euthanasia
table, why the SPCA didn't have its vets perform this service.
"No money" was again the excuse. (Today it is almost impossible to adopt an animal, especially a female, from the SPCA
without agreeing to have it neutered. This is as it should be
and is just one of the positive changes that have occurred in
the SPCAs over the years.) I urged my assistants to advise
owners that neutering was available through me. Many owners did contract with me to do the castrations at their homes
for a modest fee.

There were numerous churches of dubious authenticity in
the city, and some had strange names. I had a visitor one
morning. He was a tall, distinguished-looking black man in
minister's garb. He introduced himself as Bishop Worthington
of the "Heavenly Cloud" ministry. "I hear you make house
calls, alternating cats. I have two toms need alternating. They
stink bad."

I understood. Non-castrated male cats' (toms') urine could
become foul-smelling near maturity. They also sprayed, leaving their calling card, so to speak, to advise the females

(queens) of their presence. We arranged a date and time to "alternate" his toms at his home and church. "My fee is five dollars per cat, payable in advance," I advised the bishop, as he had told me to address him. Experience had taught me that collection after the surgery could be difficult.

"We have a neighborhood rat problem. A number of my parish members, my lambs, have cats that need to be alternated too. Suppose I round them all up. Could you reduce your fee?" I asked how many he was talking about, and surprisingly he told me ten or twelve at least. That would give me a most profitable and unusual afternoon's work.

"If you can assure me at least ten, then it would be four dollars per surgery." We agreed and shook hands. Wow! He must have a very large ministry.

The bishop was as good as his word. There were a round dozen male cats, each accompanied by its owner, all jammed into the small storefront church. Some cats were in carriers, some on leashes, some arm-held. It was pandemonium. With my collapsible operating table set up in the small altar area, there was barely room to move. We needed an organizer, a leader. The good Bishop Worthington in his dark suit and white collar took over. He directed the owners to line up. He suggested that to save time, he collect my fees and I start the surgeries. I agreed. It was obvious that it was going to take much more time than anticipated.

The procedure in those days was somewhat crude. The cat was wrapped head first in a leather, boot-like restraint. The hind legs were held by my experienced part-time assistant. The scrotal-area hair was shaved, exposing the testicles. The skin was dabbed with an antiseptic and Novocain, a local anesthetic, was injected. The surgery took only a few minutes after the cat was in the boot.

I had completed a number of surgeries before I noticed the bishop had disappeared. Suspicion set in. I questioned one of the lambs. "Oh, the bishop was called away. A sick call." I had no option but to complete the castrations, as each owner swore he or she had paid Worthington. I waited around the seedy Heavenly Cloud church for an hour, but no bishop. My suspicions were now a certainty. The shepherd had abandoned me.

First thing the next morning, I called the church. Bishop Worthington answered in his distinctive voice. The bishop, he said, was "unavailable," his whereabouts "unknown." "Tell the bishop," I exclaimed, "he owes me forty-eight dollars, and I intend to collect."

Of course, I never did. He was clever. A letter was hand-delivered to me at the SPCA. It thanked me for my assistance as a "fund-raiser" for the Heavenly Cloud ministry. I surrendered. It would have been a his-word, my-word case, with a lawyer charging me $25. Jimmy Swaggart, Tammy Faye Bakker, and Jim Bakker may have been bigger fund-raisers, but they didn't have the bishop's class. I received a special "blessing" card. It guaranteed that I would float for eternity on the "Heavenly Cloud" for my generous support.

The SPCA printed and dispersed a monthly newsletter to a large number of people in addition to "members." It was not only a news publication, but a form of fund solicitation. I offered to write a column on pet care, disease prevention, and timely medical and surgical problems. It was not altogether altruistic on my part. I needed to be exposed to as many pet owners as possible. They could not consult Dr. Scanlon if they did not know he existed.

The column proved popular. A number of people wrote describing problems and asking for advice. I kept a copy of the columns and when I first started my practice, I submitted them to the *Philadelphia Inquirer* for possible publication. The editors liked the idea and agreed to publish my column, "Pet Care," in their Sunday edition. It provided needed income and more name exposure.

Another function of the Pennsylvania SPCA was to investigate charges of animal cruelty or neglect. If our agents found sufficient grounds, they would prosecute the perpetrators. In many cases, the veterinarians were involved in the investigations and legal cases. We supplied the so-called expert testimony to the judges. Our several agents were inundated with investigations. It seemed that half the city's residents accused their neighbors of cruelty to their pets. Some complaints were valid, but most were simply caused by "neighborly" spite, dislike, or disputes.

Early on, as the last man on the vet staff, I became the court "expert," but certainly not by choice. The chief and the other vet wanted no part of the courts. It was time-consuming, and many of the cases were so sordid, so horrible, so sick and sadistic that the extra pay was no compensation. What some so-called humans can do to animals is incomprehensible. What urge would prompt a person to set animals afire with gasoline is unknown to me, and I can't understand the viciousness with which beatings were given, but this was commonplace. Then there was the depravity, which I will not describe. No reader would want to know, and fifty years later I am still trying to erase it from my mind.

Our penurious president had no budget restrictions for prosecutions. The publicity, he believed, made the SPCA look good. Donations would pour in after he alerted the news media to an especially vicious, gory case. To me, this was exploitation, but Phillips felt the ends justified the means. I guess the most frustrating part of it was that, in most cases, the guilty owners were just warned and fined. Only the most depraved went to prison.

One satisfying case was the break-up of a criminal gang that sponsored dog fights. Large sums of money were made on admissions and betting. The dogs were pitted against each other, often to the death. Can you imagine what kind of people enjoy such so-called sport? What must their hearts and souls be like, to bet on the mutilation and usually slow, painful death of a dog? Even the "victors" were terribly mangled. I despised the sponsors of such barbarism and confess to pleasure when they themselves were caged.

I saw enough cruelty cases in my year at the SPCA to last a lifetime, but I never took any of them home. To make life more bearable, I pretended they didn't happen. I believe the psychologists call it "blocking out." My court time at the SPCA was difficult. This was one of the reasons I resigned.

It was time to leave the SPCA. I had done my year's penance and I was getting out. I had received needed experience, had been exposed to every conceivable disease, wound, and accident; I had gained immeasurable confidence. Getting to know the owners, communicating with them, learning their needs, and seeing—in most of them—the pure love for their pets had been an important reward. I learned that successful medical or surgical treatment did not earn loyalty if the owner was unhappy or disliked the vet. I observed one of my assistants who was a good vet but disliked by many owners. He was cold and showed no affection for their pets.

Yes, I would miss some enjoyable things at the clinic. We had many children bring in their pets. The children were respectful, looked up to me, and hung on my every word. They were grateful to me for the care I gave their pets. The children's eyes reflected this as well as adoration for their pets and sorrow for the animals' suffering. To see the sadness leave their eyes was a constant joy to me. In a free clinic there are many children like them; in private practice there are few. I knew I would miss the children and their pets.

There was no way I could face a future of euthanizing daily ten to twenty healthy animals whose only need was to be loved; no way I could continue to dispense old-fashioned, often useless medicines; no way I could routinely be involved in those cruelty cases. The time was at hand to take the plunge and open my own hospital. My wife and I had saved some money, and I had made inquiries about possible bank financing.

I wrote a letter of resignation, with one month's notice. I handed it to Mr. Phillips. He read it and said, "Dr. Scanlon, I can't believe this. You must reconsider. We have been so pleased with your innovations, your dedication. I felt you were happy here. We need you to help us carry on our mission." He paused, dropped my letter. "Now, suppose we raise your salary to one hundred dollars a week, with another raise in three months. Would you reconsider?" Mr. "No Funds" suddenly had deep pockets.

"Mr. Phillips, I've given this a lot of thought, and it's time for me to move on." Defensively, I pointed out, "Look, I'm giving you a month's notice, lots of time to get a replacement." I wanted to part on good terms. "I'll help all I can in the interviewing; we'll find someone capable."

Mr. Phillips recognized my resolution. "Well, we're sorry to lose you." He rose, extended his hand. "We wish you all the best." We shook hands and I left.

I didn't have much respect for Mr. Phillips, the president, or for his son, who was the vice president, and certainly not for the superfluous office manager, William Dietz. It all seemed too cozy. They all drove nice society cars. Very long lunches were routine, as were three- and four-day weekends. They never inspected or visited the clinic or kennels. They were aware of but ignored the "death wagons" until I raised hell. They arrived late and left early. They took long vacations. They were "fat cats" and parasites in my book.

I believed they understated the clinic's income in the published financial statements of the annual reports. They fought most suggested improvements and resisted new medications and techniques because "the budget couldn't cover them." However, they were assiduous in raising funds. They courted many compassionate, elderly women of money. They personally opened the mail, bypassing the secretaries, and I suspected some cash contributions never reached the destinations for which they were intended.

Kathy laughed merrily when I described my disgust at the SPCA's inner workings in one of our chats. "Doc, I love you; you're refreshing, the last believer. Everyone's on the take: the politicians, the police, the ministers. Wherever there's cash, there's sticky fingers." She gave me a patronizing pat. "Do you think the M.D.'s who check my girls declare their cash fees? Do you think I declare all my cash income? What makes you think the SPCA hierarchy is any different?" She added condescendingly, "Don't be a fool, join the crooks."

I suspected she was right, but remarked, "Yes, but a lot of those crooks go to jail."

She gave her Irish grin. "Yeah, but a hell of a lot more don't. Only the stupid. Take care of yourself. No one else will." Kathy was hard-headed and practical. "You'll learn."

Yes, I was learning, but I couldn't visualize ever "learning" enough to take money at the cost of denying our dependent pets the best.

Over the years, I had many other contacts with SPCAs. Things change. Today's SPCAs are fighting the still huge unwanted pet populations head-on. They provide neutering clinics and demand adoptees be sterilized. They are efficient and do not support "fat cat" management. Their services are invaluable and deserving of all pet lovers' support.

five

Early On: I'm Adopted

Early on in my practice, house calls were very welcome. They not only earned a modestly higher fee than a clinic visit, they also frequently involved more than one patient. Hobby show-dog breeders were especially desirable clients. They usually sold their non-show-quality puppies locally. The new pet owners were often referred to the breeder's veterinarian. Most could afford and paid their vet's fees. They took the best care of their expensive, well-bred companions.

Guy Croyle was a small-time coonhound breeder who defied the usual practices of all the breeders I encountered over the years. He was one of a kind. He neither showed nor hunted the few pups he bred. He retained one or two pups from the two brood bitches he bred yearly. The others he gave away. Imagine, a breeder giving away the merchandise. Later in our relationship, he showed me his yearly advertisement in *Field and Stream.* It read "Purebred Coonhound Puppies Free to Approved Coon Hunters. Pay shipping costs only and return crate."

One early spring afternoon, I was sitting alone in my new clinic, as happened so often in that period. The idleness afforded me time to read and keep up with professional journals as well as keep the clinic spotless. A tall, fit, deeply tanned man I judged to be about forty entered. He introduced himself, "I'm Guy Croyle, nurseryman. I have a bitch with a whelping problem." He described the situation.

As I listened, I noticed there was something unusual about his coloring, which initially I had taken for a tan. He had slightly oblique black eyes and high cheekbones that stood out sharply. Later I learned they were inherited from a full-blooded Cherokee grandmother. Altogether he was a good-looking man in an exotic way.

"She needs help now." He pointed out the window to a large, open-bedded truck, whose door advertised "Guy Croyle Nurseries." I rose, sensing he was a man who expected prompt action.

"Give me a couple minutes to get some gloves, forceps, and drugs."

He nodded. "I'll be in the truck. I'll drive you back."

I copied his phone number from the truck's cab and left a note for my overdue part-time secretary. This was before my acquisition of the incomparable Mrs. Walsh.

He drove fast but carefully through a well-to-do section known as Penn Valley. His concentration discouraged conversation as he turned down River Road. About a mile from the Schuylkill River, a sign reading "Guy Croyle Nurseries" appeared. We drove on a dirt road through acres of evergreen trees and plants of many sizes and varieties. We passed an early American farmhouse and he stopped beside a huge stone barn with open equipment sheds. A large greenhouse adjoined the barn. I stared overlong at a monstrous pile of multi-sized boulders and a smaller mound of smooth, river-washed stones and flagstone. He explained, "I do landscape design, pools, fountains, patios—whatever the client or land calls for. Can't have too many rocks."

Grasping my black medical bag, I followed my large nurs-eryman into the barn. There were a few high windows that allowed in some shafts of light. The visibility overall, however, was very poor and I could barely follow the fast-striding new client. Adding to a growing eerie feeling of unreality was a great chorus of baying hounds that started as he opened another door.

The large room we entered was also poorly lighted. To the right and left of the narrow aisle were large post-and-wire pens. Each seemed to hold three or four hounds, leaping at the walls and pen doors, all seemingly in full voice. They were baying, barking, and howling and seemed determined to get to me, the intruder. It was like walking through a dreadful sound gauntlet of ghost dogs.

We reached another door and finally entered a well-lit room. Thankfully my leader closed the door, shutting out the earsplitting hounds' chorus.

In the center of the room was a good-sized whelping pen. It was occupied by a nicely conformed blue-ticked hound and three nursing pups. I looked through the clean, chopped yellow straw that filled the box. There was very little blood and no placenta or afterbirth membranes visible. She had cleaned up thoroughly. That was good, as ingestion of the afterbirth stimulated milk production and other beneficial effects.

No need to ask for a history. "Georgia's seven years old, always been healthy," Guy volunteered. "This is her fourth litter. She always has six to eight healthy pups within a few hours. This time, though, she stopped labor completely over four hours ago." He gently, fondly, patted the bitch's head. "I know she has more pups." Several tail thumps confirmed this statement.

"Get her to her feet and we'll have a look-see," I advised him, donning latex gloves. My lubricated fingers disclosed a pup jammed in the birth canal. Rather than attempt a forceps delivery, I repelled the little one. The unsanitary barn conditions were an invitation to infection. Hopefully the pup was pushed into a normal birthing position. After giving her an injection to stimulate uterine contractions, I tried to allay Guy's anxiety. "She seems in good condition and should resume her labor in twenty to thirty minutes. Everything should work out, although we'll have a dead pup." I had found mothers-in-progress do better when strangers and owners aren't hanging over them, so I suggested that we leave and come back to check her in a little while.

Guy rose from his knees, nodding agreement. "Come up to the house, have some coffee and cake . . . unless you have to go back to your office?"

I told a half-truth. "No, I'm not expecting any patients till later." If only I were.

After passing through a large living area, we came into an impressive-sized kitchen. It had a large, old-style fireplace, and antique cooking utensils hung from an oaken mantel. The kitchen table and counters were cluttered. Empty TV dinner trays, empty dog food cans, and dirty dishes covered the table, counters, and sink. The windows were grimy and the curtains frayed and greasy-looking. There was, I concluded, no Mrs. Croyle, or she was a dismal housekeeper!

"Coke or coffee," he offered.

"Coke's fine," I said, mindful of all the dirty utensils.

Reading my thoughts, Guy explained with a wry smile, "Today's Thursday. My housekeeper comes in on Fridays." He excused himself and made a series of phone calls from a nearby desk. While conversing, he made notes. He gave some orders in Spanish, which was interesting. I later found out his employees were Mexican or Puerto Rican. "No one works like immigrants," he explained. "They are hungry and willing."

Everything worked out well with Georgia. When it was over, we had six healthy, squirming, nursing pups and a self-satisfied mother. There was the one dead pup, but Guy seemed pleased with the outcome. "She should be checked tomorrow and given another prophylactic penicillin injection," I advised. "That should do it, though. She should be fine."

He drove me back to my non-patient clinic. "I'll be working in the nursery all afternoon tomorrow. Come when it's convenient; just blast your horn." The big truck rumbled off as I
congratulated myself on acquiring a new client with lots of potential patients. It appeared he had at least twenty or so adult
hounds. (Wrong. There were thirty-two!)

Friday, the following day, I had two morning patients. I remember because at that time, two constituted a busy morn.
After lunch, I headed for River Road. I again walked the
Gauntlet of Noisy Hounds and made a leisurely and thorough
exam of Georgia and family. Guy's sharp black eyes followed
my every move. My summary was satisfying. Her temperature
was normal, no infection. The uterus had involuted nicely.
She had plenty of good-quality milk and the pups were fine.
One small female had a little umbilical hernia, but that
wouldn't cause any problem. I didn't have to feign enjoyment
of examining the puppies. Few things are more appealing than
a litter of healthy, squirming hound pups. Georgia agreed with
me, and nuzzled my hand with what I chose to think was affection and appreciation. "It's unlikely I'll have to see her
again, Guy. She seems absolutely fine, and she's obviously a
good mother." Mindful of future fees, I advised him, "I'll follow up later with vaccines and worming for the pups."

Guy nodded his approval. "Come up to the house and
I'll settle up. No need to send a bill." I mentally hoped he
wouldn't need any change. My pockets were bare. I had spent
the few bills I had on a half-tank of gasoline.

His housekeeper was a gem. Except for the curtains, the
kitchen was miraculously spotless. This time when he offered
Coke or coffee, I chose coffee. The cup was clean. I sipped
slowly, with enjoyment. I was in no hurry. My part-time high-
school girl was in the office with Guy's phone number. I could
be there in ten minutes or so should a client wander in.

He was indeed a bachelor. "Not that I don't enjoy a
woman's company on occasion," he explained. "It's just that
the nursery, the plants, and the hounds keep me busy." He

chuckled. "I guess they are my surrogate family." Watching him move quickly and lightly about the kitchen, looking at his face, I could well believe his Indian connections. He placed a checkbook on the cluttered desk.

Along with his check, he gave me some advice. I had told him that my previous work had been in urban Philadelphia. "Doc, let me tell you about the Main Line. You need to study the people. They're a breed apart. They equate quality with expense and don't hesitate to pay top dollar. Your fees are too low. Do as I've done. Check your competitors' fees and charge a little more than anyone else." He paused and tapped the desk for emphasis. "It works. Croyle Nurseries is the most expensive, but perceived as the best."

He refilled our coffee cups. "Another thing: get yourself a bigger, flashier car as soon as possible. That jalopy you drive spells poor and probably not too competent to people on 'The Line.'" He offered other constructive insights into the residents' likes and dislikes. "And one more thing. Your clinic badly needs to be landscaped."

I laughed. "Yes, I know, but big cars and good landscaping cost money. I'm a little short in that department." An understatement. I had mortgage payments due on a very small house and the clinic. What with insurance and carefully managed living expenses, I was in no way ready for a fancy car or landscaping. What money came in was spent the minute I touched it.

I had stocked my clinic with drugs on credit from the Lentz Drug Company. Dr. Lentz was our professor of pharmacology at the vet school and he also ran a drug company. Being a good businessman, he was generous in giving new graduates drugs on credit as well as needed equipment. When I remember that hungry period, it is often with wonder at how we managed to make so little money go so far. Fortunately, I was blessed with an understanding and supportive wife.

As my friendship with Guy grew through our visits it seemed he was, in a sense, adopting me. I was acquiring an older brother. True, his lifestyle was a little strange, especially all those hounds, but his desire to help my professional welfare appeared to be very sincere. He seemed to read my thoughts at times. "I love those hounds. No, I don't hunt them, but they have a two-acre fenced play pen. The neighbors hate the dogs—and me—but I'm zoned and grandfathered in, so they can't bother me." He was a trifle defensive. "Sure, caring and feeding over thirty hounds is expensive and time-consuming, but I enjoy it." Guy's dogs were a known neighborhood nuisance. Though confined, they had powerful voices. He was at constant war with the neighbors. Anyone who has heard a pack of hounds in full voice would not be blamed for siding with the neighbors.

He was also passionate about his other love. "Doc, there's nothing like taking bare ground and creating a beautiful landscape. Evergreens and flowering plants here and there, a fountain, a fish pond. All blended in with stone walls, flagstone walks, a gazebo. It's a form of creating, creating lasting beauty."

Those thoughts were interspersed with an occasional suggestion to gain new clients. "The Rotary Club is a good source of contacts, and when you can afford it, you want to join a good country club." He was a loner and eccentric, but I couldn't help liking Guy. He was offering friendship and patronage. I could use both.

His hobby hounds helped my slim income. The fees for routine care were welcome. The surgical fees for unnecessary bite wounds were not. For someone who was genuinely fond of his dogs, Guy had one peculiar belief that I never came to understand. He called it "nature's way." He refused to castrate his male hounds or to separate the females when in season. This caused Darwin's "survival of the fittest" to go into action. When one of his bitches went into heat, the males literally tore into each other, requiring surgical repairs. It also made identifying exact parentage a guess.

My protests that the bite wounds could be avoided and

were unnecessary made no impression on Guy. "Doc, you above all should believe in nature. It's nature taking its course." His ideas on canine reproduction frustrated and perplexed me. We just didn't agree on those kennel practices. "I believe in nature's way. It produces stronger pups. A few bite wounds are just part of the process."

After repairing some very nasty punctures caused again by the males fighting over a bitch in heat, I decided this had to stop. Regardless of Guy's theories on natural selection and survival of the fittest, permitting this to happen was wrong. I decided to have it out with Guy.

Let's skip all the great arguments and appeals on humane grounds that I made to him. His face assumed a frozen, set look at the end of my requests. "And you want me to castrate all but the breeding males, and they are to be confined and hand bred only." The black eyes flashed.

"Yes, Guy," I answered, equally glum-faced. "They will be contented and not continually upset and fighting. It's more . . ."

He interrupted, "Yeah, more humane." Guy looked directly at me. "Doc, we are each entitled to our opinions. Friends often disagree."

I interrupted him. "Guy, answer me. Are you saying no? Sounds like you are." Guy looked at his shoes. "Let me say this," I continued, and trying unsuccessfully to keep my voice level, I repeated, "let me say this. If you won't be reasonable and cut out these barbaric practices, you'll need a new veterinarian."

Guy gave me a piercing look. With a flushed face, he turned and left me staring at a large, strong back.

I heard nothing from Guy. Two days passed and I was on the point of calling him and mentioning that I still had SPCA connections. I was determined and would use every threat or plea available. I had no intention of giving up even if it cost a friend and a client.

To my great pleasure and surprise, my weighty problem was suddenly solved. "Dr. Scanlon, I meant to tell you yesterday that a Mr. Croyle called and asked you to call him about a number of dogs he wants castrated." My part-time, nice but air-headed secretary (pre–Mrs. Walsh) was fumbling at the desk. "Now I wrote his number down. It must be here somewhere."

I smiled. "That's okay, Gloria. I have his number." Gee, she really wasn't such a bad secretary after all.

During this period I welcomed occasional part-time relief work at the SPCA. One day in early May, I spent the morning there relieving a flu-smitten colleague and returned to my mortgaged clinic around two in the afternoon. I looked in astonishment at the exterior. The patchy lawn had been sodded with lush, green grass. Evergreen bushes of various sizes had been tastefully placed along the sides and front area. Stone flower boxes, with concrete car-protecting slabs, had been built in front of my six-car parking area. (I remember wondering at the time if it would ever be full. At that moment I was incapable of visualizing the battles I would wage with zoning boards and neighboring businesses in my quest for a desperately needed two dozen more spots.) The boxes were ablaze with spring flowers. What a marvelous transformation, from the dowdy to a statement of beauty, taste, and success— or at least of caring.

A few carefully placed vari-colored boulders left the Croyle signature. A departing nursery truck driven by a straw-hatted Puerto Rican or Mexican laborer confirmed the source of design and plantings. Who else?

"Guy Croyle Nurseries," he answered on my fifth ring.

"My God, I can't believe what you've done. It's beautiful! It's day from night, but . . ."

A laugh from Guy. "Doc, I know you can't afford it. You'll be billed at cost only, and take as long as you want, installments, whatever."

"But Guy," I started to protest.

"Doc, listen. You couldn't drive by a sick dog day after day and not try to help it. Well, I had to help your sick, no-landscape clinic. It was a personal affront. You're my friend." He sounded like a big brother. "I've told you how important appearances are on the Main Line."

Many compliments came after the face-lift. Certainly some new clients were attracted. One well-to-do matron asked who had done such "a tasteful design." "Did you say Guy Croyle? He's a kook. He refused to give me an estimate on a new garden. I got a lecture. He claimed I didn't properly feed or water my present one. A real crazy. He wasn't going to 'let me abuse his children.'" I grinned. That fit Guy.

Shortly after that episode, while I was vaccinating his unruly hounds, Guy dropped a bomb. "I'm going to be married, and I need a best man. Are you free June twelfth?" My mouth probably opened without sound. "Just a few friends and family—the bride's—at the farmhouse," Guy continued.

I knew he had no family. He had once confided that at fifteen, he had run away from an abusive father. "I never went back. The old SOB is probably dead."

"I'd be honored. Who's the lucky lady?"

"Why, Ed, it's Maria, of course. Who else?"

Maria was about thirty years old. She answered the nursery phone and kept his books on a part-time basis. She was attractive in a dark, fragile, Mediterranean way. She seemed shy and spoke very little on the few occasions we met. Maria was the only woman, aside from clients, in Guy's sphere that I knew of. Hooray for Guy! He needed and deserved more than his hounds and a lonesome, workaholic life.

About five months after the quiet ceremony, he had another surprising announcement. "Maria's pregnant!" I congratulated him and shook his hand with the obligatory male back slap. But it was apparent he was anything but happy with his news. I asked how Maria was faring.

The dark eyes appeared clouded, his expression somber. "Physically, she's fine. Mentally, she's sick." He sat down. "Not long after we were married, I found out she had been hospitalized several times. Manic-depressive was the diagnosis." He sighed and cracked his big knuckles. "She always seemed fairly normal, maybe too quiet at times. Actually, we didn't have much of a courtship. You know how many hours I put on the job."

He looked at his hand and confessed. "It's an old story, Ed. We had an affair and she became pregnant. I was lonesome and I wanted our child to have a legit father." Another sigh. "When she's in her manic phase, she's destructive and dangerous, mostly to herself. But with a baby? God, I'll be afraid to leave the house."

"What does the doctor say?" I asked.

"That's the hell of it. Maria doesn't understand and if anything, blames the doctor. She won't see him anymore and refuses the medication."

My heart went out to him as I envisioned the picture and guessed the future. "Can I do anything?"

He rose, extended his hand. "Just what you're doing, lending me a shoulder. I have to talk to someone." I felt sad as he left. He would need more than a shoulder.

Not long after his baby son was born, Maria was hospitalized. "Even with a full-time, live-in nanny, I couldn't handle it," he revealed. "I had to have her committed, to protect little Guy." His love and care for his son were touching. He gave up all but a few of his favorite hounds. "They take up too much of my time from my boy."

Unfortunately, Maria periodically became ill. The diagnosis was now chronic schizophrenia. There was no cure and little meaningful therapy then other than confinement. Guy rarely discussed her condition, nor did I ask. The suddenly aging lines on his face, however, reflected her poor diagnosis. He looked ten years older than his true age of forty-six.

Did you ever look back and wonder how and why you lost a good friend? In Guy's case, I was mostly to blame for our drifting apart. Early on, I wasn't that busy and enjoyed his dropping by the clinic for long and short chats. Over time, there just wasn't enough freedom for me to socialize there with him. He would wait in the small reception area awhile and then leave. I should have explained and made time to meet with him. I should have known he might be offended by my new unavailability.

At any rate, we gradually drifted apart. His veterinary needs were almost nil after his kennel reduction. I should have been alerted he was writing me off when his nursery help brought his dogs in for care. Eventually even they disappeared. We were both too busy and stiff-necked to talk and repair the situation. It is one of my regrets.

We just never got together. I heard reports of his increasing eccentricity, and then he disappeared. I do know Guy lived long enough to see his son through college. My daughter Patricia attended the same college as Guy Jr.

Friendship, like Guy's beloved plants, needs attention. I lost my Indian brother, mostly through neglect.

six

Inspector General— Canine Royalty

To paraphrase Will Rogers, I never met a dog I didn't like. But like humans, some were easier to like than others, and Inspector General was one of my favorites. There was a lot to like about him—he not only brought me considerable vet's fees and numerous referrals, but he also introduced me to a new (to me) and exciting sport, bird dog field trials. Beyond that, he was a beautiful specimen of the English setter field dog, white with black ear and body patches and the characteristic tick-like markings. With his regal, upright head and imperious pose, he seemed to say, "Look at me. I'm special." And he was.

The General was first brought into my office under unusual conditions. I knew something was up from the moment Mrs. Walsh gave me a knowing look. His owner proclaimed, as he entered the exam room, that he was Anthony Imbesi in such a way that I knew I was supposed to recognize the name. He lived in Bucks County, far out of my usual territory. "Do you mind if I ask why you brought him to me? It's quite a drive to have a dog examined."

"My mother lives nearby," he explained. "You take care of her miniature poodle, Pierre." I mentally ran through my list of poodle Pierres, of which there were many. Suddenly I made the connection. Mrs. Walsh had told me on one of his mother's yearly visits that she was the matriarch of the 7-Up dynasty. Anthony himself was nothing less than the CEO of the "un-cola" company.

"I see," was all I could reply.

"Anyway, I have nothing to lose by bringing him to you. My vet in Bucks County can't find anything wrong with him." Anthony's temper, which I was to come to know well, showed a little. "This dog was a champion, won trial after trial. I paid four grand for him, and now he's not worth a damn. And they say there's nothing wrong with him!"

Four grand seemed like a lot to lay out for a bird dog, even a champion, and that was in Eisenhower-era dollars. It was an especially large sum since Anthony's dog competed in amateur events where there was no cash prize, only a trophy. But the well-off owners were very competitive and willing to spend top dollar for a proven winner.

"What do you mean, he's not worth a damn?" The General, as he sat there on my stainless-steel table, moving his eyes from face to face as we talked, looked like the textbook illustration of a healthy dog. His owner was equally fit-looking. Suntanned, with a heavily muscled body and the coal-black hair and eyes of his Mediterranean ancestors, altogether a good-looking man. If he had been six inches taller, he would have been striking.

"He just doesn't perform. I've won one trial since I bought him, and since then he's disgraced me every time. I've had vets at home and vets at the trials—I've had everybody examine him, and they all say nothing's wrong. I know the dog has courage and talent, and I've been around dogs long enough to know something has to be wrong. If you can't help me, I'm going to have to try a witch doctor."

"What did the other vets do by way of examination?"

"Everything! X-rays, blood work, physicals. Specimens of everything that goes into or comes out of that dog went to the lab. All negative, negative!"

Stalling for time while I thought, I started doing a routine physical. It wasn't likely every vet he consulted was incompetent, or if they were, it was a sad comment on my profession. The General's heart and lung sounds were normal, his eyes clear in the ophthalmoscope, mucous membranes a healthy pink. After five minutes of close scrutiny I found nothing abnormal.

I could think of only one thing to do that the previous vets hadn't already done several times over. "Mr. Imbesi, I'd like to see the General in action and do an exam in the field. Something must be happening to him when he performs that doesn't show up at rest." Anthony looked surprised, giving me the feeling I was on new territory.

"Fine. At my farm? I'll write you directions. I'm in Bucks County near New Hope," he said, naming an area of fabulous multimillion-dollar farms.

"Yes. Does Sunday morning suit you? Around ten o'clock?"

"All right," he said. "I'll have a horse ready for you."

As Sunday approached, I started to get a little nervous. Although I was an experienced rider, it had been a long time since I had been on horseback and I wasn't really in riding shape. I didn't look forward to the prospect of nursing my bruised muscles Monday morning. And I was concerned about my ability to find what was wrong with the General. I felt I could, but only Sunday would tell.

When I arrived at the farm, I knew that on the sore muscle worry at least, I would be okay. A fine Tennessee walking horse was waiting for me, a representative of the breed famous for its comfortable ride. Anthony, already mounted, and Inspector General were waiting, along with another dog and a mounted handler. Anthony wanted to simulate actual trial conditions as closely as possible, so the General would be running with a brace mate. As soon as I was mounted, Anthony and our entourage started off for the fields where we would watch the General hunt.

As soon as he was released, Inspector General started hunting with an enthusiasm and excitement that showed how very much he loved to do what he was bred for. He made a big cast and kept up his good performance for about fifteen minutes. That fifteen minutes was all it took to hook me on field trials for life. I had rarely seen such an exhibition of animals doing what they were bred to do, with pleasure and eagerness.

"Here he goes," Anthony said. "Do you see the way he's slowing down?"

By twenty minutes, even my untutored eye could see the dog was faltering. "Call him back now, please."

I dismounted, stethoscope in hand, and approached the General. I stooped to begin my examination, and the cause was evident as soon as I looked inside his mouth. "Mr. Imbesi," I said triumphantly, "I think I've found the problem."

"What? So easily?"

"His soft palate is swelling up and becoming elongated." I showed Anthony the back of the General's throat, where the swollen palate (the soft back of the roof of the mouth) was clearly partially blocking his throat. There hadn't been a hint of the problem in my earlier examination, and probably not in the other vets' either. By the time he reached a vet, he'd had a chance to cool down and the swelling had subsided. The problem was also probably exacerbated by an allergic reaction to some field grass, which I could treat with an antiallergen.

"No wonder he runs out of gas," Anthony said. "Is it treatable?"

"I should be able to correct the problem with surgery."

"Really? He could win again?" he asked. Then: "Is there any risk? I'm really attached to this guy."

I explained that there was always an element of risk to anything requiring the patient to be put under anesthesia, but that this was a fairly safe operation and the chances for a full recovery were excellent.

"Damn them, they thought they had me, took me for a pigeon by selling me a lemon." Though Anthony's words were angry, he was smiling and his tone was triumphant. "We'll show 'em, Doc. I'll take that lemon and win every trial I put him in. Take him back with you, cure him, and you can name your price."

Well, Inspector General soon returned to his winning ways. Nearly invincible in the amateur events and a beauty in the field, he was something to be proud of. And Anthony didn't forget who had made it possible. Whenever he was asked what had caused the great turnaround, he always said it wouldn't have been possible without Doc Scanlon.

One day, after the General had been winning again for a few months, Mrs. Walsh announced a call from a professional dog handler in Virginia. "Doctor Scanlon," the man greeted me, "I'm sending a dog to you. An English pointer. He'll be arriving at the Philadelphia airport tomorrow at ten A.M."

I was confused. "What? A dog? What for?"

"Our vet down here can't find anything wrong with him. His complete history and medical records will be with him."

It seemed that thanks to Anthony's help and recommendation, I had developed a reputation for being a miracle worker, a court of last appeals for hunting dogs' obscure problems. I received many such calls and telegrams in the months and years that followed, and collecting dogs at the airport became a chore for Mrs. Walsh or a kennel person.

As I was in most cases considered the final authority, I could charge almost whatever I wanted. The struggle wasn't over, but I was a long way from raising Dalmatian pups in a closet for expenses. These moneyed clients were accustomed to paying well—and on time! Their fees more than made up for the clients who couldn't or wouldn't pay on time, and I ultimately managed to make college educations available to my four girls, partly on the largesse of my wealthy clients. The year I had three daughters in college at one time was rough, though!

Due to my success in treating the General, I became the sole veterinary practitioner for Anthony's Willow Bend Farm Kennels. He had, at one time, over a hundred dogs: puppies, brood bitches, and trial dogs. He and his staff took excellent care of the dogs, and I saw them mostly for routine care—worming, vaccinating, periodic physical exams and lab work, monitoring their diets, and so on. But as anyone who raises animals knows, no matter how good the preventive care, sooner or later some animals will get sick. In my second year of veterinary attendance at Willow Bend Farm, all hell broke loose.

Anthony's bitches whelped about forty pups that year, a record number. I was there many days, helping with difficult deliveries and administering distemper vaccines. Our vaccine against that most dreaded of canine killers was pretty good—not as good as those we have today, but the best available at the time. It was a satisfactory protection against the virus of Carre, known as distemper, which was that era's main killer and maimer of dogs.

When the last litter was born and vaccinated, I was looking forward to the chance to stay away from the farm for a while. It was good business, and I had grown close to Anthony and his staff, but it was quite a drive. It took already scarce time from my fast-growing practice.

Six days into my hiatus, I got a call from Anthony's kennel master. "Those last three litters you saw don't look too good, Doc," he said.

"What's wrong?"

"No appetite, cough, elevated temperatures, diarrhea, vomiting. None of them seems to have any life at all."

I prayed I was wrong, but I felt it was distemper. It could show up in many forms, but that was the chief catalog of early symptoms. "I'll be there tonight, after I close the hospital."

When I examined the pups that night, I knew my fears

were right. It was a full-blown outbreak of the virus, and all nineteen pups were seriously sick.

"It's distemper, isn't it," the kennel master said. It wasn't really a question.

"I'm afraid it is. They must have already been incubating the virus when I vaccinated them. There's no cure, so all I can do is treat the symptoms and hope for the best." I didn't mention that the "best" would be to have even a small number of pups left alive. Anyone who worked with dogs professionally knew, by reputation if not by experience, the nightmare that was distemper. There was also a good chance that some of the surviving dogs would be disabled in some way, leaving them unable to perform in field trials.

"Tony," he said ominously, "is not going to be pleased."

Over the past two years of comparatively good dog health, I had had only a few opportunities to see Anthony's infamous temper in action, and rarely directed toward me. I had a feeling that lack would be more than made up for when I next heard from him. Fortunately, he was out that night, and I was spared having to tell him face to face. I administered near-useless drugs to each of the unfortunate puppies and went home.

"Anthony Imbesi's on line one, Doctor. He sounds furious." Mrs. Walsh spoke the words I had been dreading all morning.

I took two deep breaths and picked up the phone. "Hello, Tony."

"I hope you have malpractice insurance." Nice greeting.

"Wait, Tony—" I tried to explain how the dogs must have been sick when I inoculated them, but he cut me off.

"I don't blame you, Ed. The drug company's at fault. But my lawyer says I can't sue them unless I sue you too." He was trying to control himself.

"It isn't the company's fault, either. Lederle Laboratories, the company that made the vaccine, is considered the best. They test all the vaccine before shipping," I offered.

"I don't care about that," Anthony interrupted. "We didn't have a sick dog on the farm before you gave them that injection, and now I've got three dead pups and sixteen more than halfway there. I'm not going to swallow this kind of loss." He was deaf to all attempts to explain. "The three litters were worth at least eight hundred dollars per puppy, and that's without factoring in the lost breeding potential and prize money. This is going to be one big suit."

"Tony, with all this going on," I had to ask, "do you want to have another vet treat the pups that are left? And your other dogs?"

"No. I already told you, I don't blame you. I'll do what I can to keep you out of any bad publicity, and tell everybody that I only sued you because I had to. When they see you're still my vet, they'll believe me. Some men from Lederle are coming down here tomorrow to look at the pups. I want you to be here." Anthony was furious, but fair and loyal.

The next day when I pulled into Willow Bend Farm, Anthony was standing outside the kennels, involved in an obviously heated discussion with two men in gray suits. "My company has strict quality control, too, but if someone shows up with foreign material in the bottle, we pay them! That's what liability insurance is for." Anthony's arms were moving like a windmill.

The older of the two men said—and from his tone of voice, not for the first time—"If our vaccine proves to be at fault, we will gladly pay the replacement value of the animals. We are simply telling you how unlikely that is."

"Well, sure it's unlikely, if you're the ones doing the testing." Anthony's words made me remember Mrs. Allesandroni, when it was necessary to autopsy her Doberman. "I want an independent lab to do the testing."

The older gray suit said, "We only did the preliminary testing. Samples have been sent to two independent labs. We'll just have to wait for their results."

The rest of their visit was only a formality. They confirmed my diagnosis and left the farm, leaving me with a steaming Anthony. "They want a fight, I'll give them one."

The next few weeks were a haze of sleepless nights and days spent either at the farm, driving to the farm, or trying to get a few hours with my other patients between visits. I hardly saw my family at all and was constantly on the receiving end of Anthony's verbal abuse. He had to let off steam, and I was the closest target.

But the worst part was watching the puppies, one by one, sicken and die. Four of them had to be put down because of chorea, or Saint Vitus's dance, which causes convulsions and uncontrolled twitching of the limbs. This, caused by damage to the brain and nervous system, is distemper's most horrifying terminal outcome. I was not a happy camper.

The only bright spot was that Lederle Labs' excellent team of lawyers agreed to represent me at no cost. At the one pretrial meeting I attended it was clear that they weren't planning to pay a cent in damages, and I was glad they had decided not to throw me on Anthony's mercy.

"We cannot allow a precedent to be set that would support pet owners in suing us whenever a vaccinated dog dies. The test showed that the vaccine was perfectly safe. This was just one of those things."

I did manage to share a piece of information that was helpful to our case. "Tony has dogs coming and going all the time, to and from trials all over North America. Any one of them could have carried the virus back to the farm."

"There you have it. The pups were sick when you inoculated them. No one was to blame, and the vaccine may even have helped the survivors."

"I don't think Tony is going to accept that."

"Let him not accept it," one of the younger lawyers said, "as long as the judge does."

The chief counsel said sternly, "We hope to avoid a trial, if at all possible."

Amen to that!

The storm stopped as suddenly as it had begun. On one of my visits, Anthony informed me that the suit was over. "My lawyers told me Lederle Labs have an ironclad case. Even though they are in the wrong, there's no way to prove it. That stuff from the independent labs is going to be just too convincing for a jury."

"Well," I said while mentally doing a dance of joy, "maybe it's better this way. Save yourself some time, money, and aggravation."

When all the dogs had recovered or been euthanized, my next concern was how I would be paid. I had put in hundreds of hours, virtually lived at the farm, neglected my practice and family. Though Anthony had dropped the suit, he was far from content with the situation. As far as he was concerned, it was still the vaccine that had killed his dogs. I was reluctant to present him with the hefty bill for my mostly useless care. Fortunately, Lederle Labs called me one day and told me that, as a public relations gesture, the company would pay me for my time and expenses in the case.

After that, things gradually returned to normal. Anthony continued to be my biggest client and a friend, and I continued to be the Willow Bend dogs' sole veterinarian. The only change was that now brood bitches and pups were kept isolated from the trial dogs.

About six months later I was having lunch in Anthony's house. He had asked me to stay, saying he had something he wanted to talk to me about. (There was a rumor that the 7-Up King served his own product exclusively. I can't say if that is true, but it did fill the glasses every time I dined with him.) During the meal we exchanged pleasantries and field trial talk. But when the plates had been cleared, he dropped a conversational bomb. "Do you know how much I spent with you last year?"

I hoped this wasn't going to be a discussion of my rates. "No, not exactly. But you are my biggest client, so I'm sure it was a lot."

"Well over thirty-five thousand dollars." He tapped the

table for emphasis. "Now here's my proposal. I want you to sell your practice and come work for me full time. I'll have my broker help you invest the proceeds from the sale of your house and practice, and you'll get a nice farmhouse, rent-free, and thirty-five a year. I know what I paid you last year wasn't all profit, so with that and other considerations, you'll be a lot better off."

I tried to interject, but he raised his 7-Up glass and continued. "Hear me out. You'll be my farm manager and resident vet for the dogs only. I'll retain someone else for the horses." He had a small string of racehorses. "You have two daughters, don't you?"

I nodded. Three and four had yet to arrive.

"Think about it. You'll be working shorter hours, so you'll have more family time. And with a house right on the property, you can see them during the day." He paused for a response.

"Well, I don't know. I never thought of working for anyone before." I enjoyed the independence of owning my practice and the variety of patients I saw. I would lose all that if I accepted Anthony's offer. But didn't I owe it to my wife and girls to take the more secure position, my own preferences aside?

Anthony looked as though he had expected me to jump at the opportunity to be in the employ of such a titan. "You would have a two-year renewable contract, health and life insurance provided by 7-Up. You don't get many offers like that. This is quite an opportunity."

"Let me think it over, talk with my wife." I stood up to leave, my head full of confusion.

"I don't expect you to decide right away, but keep in mind this is an offer most vets would jump at. Don't take too long."

During the ride back to my hospital, my head cleared and I read between the lines. He was warning me that, if I didn't take his offer, I would be losing the substantial fees I got from him. That would be quite a blow, but I thought with my growing client base, I could handle it. Yet the idea of more time with my family, and more security, was tempting.

Then I realized that the prospect he had dangled in front
of me was a sham. Doing the jobs of both farm manager and
vet, I would have to put in nearly as many hours as I did now,
if not more. I would have to put up with Anthony's temper all
the time, and if I didn't pretend to like it, he could fire me or
just decide not to renew the contract. Several years down the
road I could be faced with the daunting task of trying to start
a new practice from scratch (and surely I wouldn't be able to
get Mrs. Walsh back!), or the humiliating one of applying for
a job in someone else's practice. When I pulled into my parking space at my hospital, where the shingle with my name
hung on my (mortgaged) porch, I made my final decision. The
next day, I called Anthony, thanked him for his kind offer, and
declined it.

Sure enough, I soon found out Anthony had hired a new
full-time vet and farm manager. He was a promising, recent
vet school graduate, with more training than I in dealing with
horses. He could see to the needs of Anthony's modest racing
stable in addition to caring for the dogs and being the farm
manager. It seemed Anthony had found a better deal—today,
they call it downsizing. It was very unlikely he was paying the
young man $35,000, and he wouldn't have to deal with any
pesky ideas about independence. It seemed like a good idea
for Anthony.

When I turned over the farm's medical records, the new vet
seemed to be a very pleasant young fellow. Some years later I
met him at a seminar. He had left Anthony's employ—apparently they had had a difference of opinion over a matter of
equine health, and he had resigned. I was sympathetic but in
no way surprised.

Although I was no longer the sole veterinarian attending
Willow Bend Farm, Anthony still brought his "problem"
cases to me. Over the years, we were friends—but as important, we were bird dog lovers.

seven

Field Trials — the Test of Champions

I never had any exposure to bird dog field trials before my association with Anthony Imbesi. My appreciation of and pleasure in them is just one more thanks I owe him. I started going to trials in hopes of seeing some dogs I had treated, especially Inspector General, perform. This is what those great dogs were bred for, and it is always uplifting to see an animal excelling at what it was born and trained to do. Their endurance, athleticism, and sense of smell were simply astonishing. On a windy, cold day, one of these marvelous dogs could point to quarry 50 to 75 feet away—a little quail, weighing less than a pound, hidden deep in underbrush. Every time I witnessed the General in competition, I felt a renewed appreciation for his beauty, superb sense of smell, and statuesque points. It felt very gratifying to know that I had a small part in his many victories.

I appreciated the pure spectacle of a trial. Participants arrived from all over the United States and even Canada to compete. Some people had only one or two superb dogs, others six or eight. A few, such as the famous King Ranch, had as many as a dozen. Some owners flew in for the day. Their hired handlers took care of the animals. Other owners stayed for the duration. The trials were always held near a good hotel that served as a base camp and put up those who stayed there in style. It was exciting; it was glamorous; it was expensive!

In the major trials, which featured a cash reward (or purse), owners did not receive the money. They took home only the sought-after trophy, which meant more to them anyway; the cash prize went to their professional trainer/handler. In amateur trials, the sole reward was the trophy, and it was hotly contested and desired.

Field trials are a sport that includes men, beautiful fields and countryside, horses, dogs, and birds, all in harmony. In a field trial, dogs are "put down" in braces; that is, two dogs are released at a time, each with a mounted handler who is either the amateur owner or a professional, depending on the type of trial.

A judge, also on horseback, accompanies each dog. A separate judge is required for every dog because the dogs cover so much ground in making their "casts," searching for pheasant or quail—often miles, and just as often in different directions. These dogs can really move, and the only way to move with them is on horseback.

When the dog finds a bird, it goes "on point," freezing in position, usually with a foreleg held up and tail erect. Then the handler dismounts and flushes the bird by swinging a flushing whip into the bushes or vegetation where the bird is hiding. When the bird takes flight, the handler shoots at it using a gun loaded with blanks. The dog is expected to hold its point until the bird has gone since the judges require a dog to be "steady to shot and wing." If the dog moves under gunshot, it loses points.

I admire the fraternity of rule makers in this sport for mandating that no birds be killed. Very early on, birds frequently were shot and killed or wounded. When this was deemed inhumane and unnecessary, it was decided that the dogs could demonstrate and exhibit their talent and hunting ability without the sacrifice of our feathered beauties.

Each brace is given a time limit—usually a half-hour, or as long as an hour in some major trials—and the winner is the dog with the most proven productive points. No fair pointing when there's no bird! Of course, the dogs are also judged on their casts, hunting patterns, style, and desire.

Another element that adds to the difficulty is that the dogs are required to "honor" each other's points. For example, dog one comes upon a quail and points. Dog two might come over the hill after the same scent. Dog two must drop behind dog one when he goes on point; otherwise, the judge does not know which dog came upon the scent first. Stealing another dog's point by taking the lead position is punished by deductions or expulsion. The dogs' intelligence shows in this challenge, as their instinct is to get as close as possible to the quarry.

Depending on the number of entries, a trial may last several days to a week. On which day, and at what time, the dog competes is as important in field trials as position is in a horse race. Just as the inside rail position is preferred in horse racing because it gives the shortest route around the track, dog owners hope for an early go because it provides more-abundant and less-wary game. By the fourth or fifth day of a major trial, the field has been hunted many times, driving away some of the birds.

In my day in the sport, the order of competition was decided fairly, by random drawing. At the end of a fancy dinner with a few libations, the night before the trial began, each dog's name was put in a bowl. Two slips were drawn at a time, and the dogs whose names were drawn together would compete at the same time, and in the order in which their names were drawn.

I admit I was hooked, and wanted to compete myself, so I bought an English setter bitch named Paoli Miss from Anthony, who was devoted to the English setter, preferring it over the more common and more successful short-haired English pointer. At first I had a lot of fun competing with Paoli Miss, even though we had little success. It was enjoyable just to be there, even though I had no chance of actually winning a trial. I was listening to and learning all the basics from the old-timers and pros.

Missy, as we called Paoli Miss, was an excellent trial dog to cut my trial teeth on. She was eager, good-tempered, easy to deal with, healthy, and she traveled well. While on the trial circuit she stayed with Paul Walker, my professional trainer/handler, and the rest of the time she lived at home in a kennel I had built under shade trees.

Field trial dogs really aren't good family pets. All they do when they're not hunting is sleep and dream about hunting. There are exceptions, of course, but generally, they aren't that interested in people as companions. My girls had a hard time understanding why Missy wouldn't let them dress her up in clothes, like all our other animals did. (Even the rabbit had to put up with it, and my youngest, Mary, once tried to dress one of the bantam roosters in a hat, with results we still laugh about.)

After a year or so, I was bitten by the "winning bug" and started thinking about upgrading to a dog with potential. I asked Paul Walker what he thought about Missy's chances, and let him know I wanted a dog that might win.

Besides his incredible harmony with the dogs, Paul had three outstanding qualities. First, he was the most handsome man I ever saw, as handsome as any movie star. Women were stunned when they met him, but he was largely unaware of his impact. He was a happily married family man who just happened to make women stare when he was around.

Second, he was the proverbial "man of few words." Paul measured his words as if they would come out of his salary. He never used a sentence when a word would do and never bothered with words if he could nod or point.

Third, he was honest. Some trainers and handlers charged for work that wasn't done, and if you asked one of them to find you a dog, he'd pocket a "finder's fee" secretly paid by the seller. Because of this practice, their recommendations were often overpriced, poor-quality dogs. Paul wouldn't have any part of that kind of thing.

"Spinning wheels," he said. "Eyes open." This, once you had learned Paul's abbreviated language, translated into "You're right, Ed. You're just spinning your wheels with Paoli Miss. I'll keep my eyes open and let you know when I find a promising candidate for you."

"Remember," I said, "I can't spend too much." The amount I could afford would have been a ridiculously large amount for a family dog, but pocket change compared with what the wealthier owners could lay out.

Nod from Paul. "Skip all-age, gamble young." Which meant "I agree with you. Good all-age [non-puppies] dogs are out of sight money-wise, when you can even find one somebody's willing to sell. We'll look at younger dogs. It's more of a gamble, but you'll have a better chance of getting a good dog for what you can afford that way."

"Fine," I said happily, glad to know I had taken a step toward actually winning a dog trial.

Paul said, "Slow." Translation: "It's not going to be quick, Ed. With the money you have to spend, and your determination to have a winner, it might take some looking to find just the right dog. Be patient."

In the end, it took about eight months of his looking. I had begun to suspect Paul had forgotten by the time he called me. "Clarence Edwards," he said. "Two Junior All-Age."

Wow, I thought. Clarence Edwards actually had two pups—I recognized his name as the owner of some really top dogs. And as they were about to graduate to the next class, they would already have had some trial experience. Finally, after all that waiting, a prospect. "Do you have a preference?" I asked Paul.

"The Builder. Stratoliner cheaper. Flip." Paul, for him, was very enthusiastic. He liked The Builder a little more but felt that both were fine dogs. Paul thought I would be happy with either. He said I could flip a coin, they were both that good.

I called Mr. Edwards immediately. After explaining who I was and what I wanted, I hesitantly asked the price of the dogs. "The Builder's two thousand, and Stratoliner's fifteen hundred." This was in Eisenhower, late-'50s, dollars.

Even the cheaper dog was five hundred more than I felt I could afford. But I listened to Mr. Edwards's pitch anyway, hoping something would come to me.

"These two dogs are littermates, and both sire and dam are by Fast Delivery." Fast Delivery was a very well-known sire, who was not only a champion himself but had already fathered many others. Such incestuous matings were not uncommon, though they were risky. Breeders hoped to get offspring with all of the common ancestor's good qualities and none of the poor ones. Inbreeding was done only when a potential reward was greater than the risk. But it was chancy, with no guarantees.

"What's your best price?" I asked hopefully.

"You just heard it."

Thinking fast, I said, "Tell you what. I'll pay you sixteen hundred for Stratoliner, a hundred more than you are asking."

"No problem," Edwards replied, his tone implying that he had no moral compunctions about taking money from someone who was clearly unbalanced.

"Just one thing," I added. "I'll give you a thousand now, and another three hundred the first two times he wins a trial."

"Don't know 'bout that." He was starting to sound like Paul Walker.

"If he's as good as you say, then you aren't taking any risk," I pressed.

"What if he gets sick or injured?"

"In that case," I assured him, "I'll pay the balance immediately."

"How do I know you won't just take the dog and run?"

"Paul Walker will vouch for me. Besides, what good would he be to me if I couldn't enter him without being arrested for theft?"

"All right. Send the thousand, and if Walker vouches for you, you'll get the dog."

When I told my wife what I had done, she told me that, even if we had to mortgage the house again, she wanted me to have that dog. And that $1,600 turned out to be some of the best money I ever spent. Only the payment of hospital bills when my daughters were born even comes close. Stratoliner (who was called Bob around the kennel) gave me years of enjoyment. It was stimulating to compete with him, and to relive his successes was a great strategy for relaxation. Like most field trial bird dogs, he wasn't much on affection. He was away frequently, so there wasn't time to bond with him like a family pet, and by nature, he preferred the kennel to the house. The times he and I were together were when we were working together, training in the field, and of course at trials.

Hunting was Stratoliner's life, what he was bred and trained for. On one occasion he was being taken off the truck after an eight-hour drive following a trial in Canada. There was food and water waiting for him in his kennel, a bitch in heat was nearby, and Paul was patting him and praising him for being such a good dog. He ignored food, water, the bitch, and Paul to follow his instinct to hunt. He took off running. We chased after him, whistling and calling his name. When we finally caught up to him in a field he was on point. Fortunately he had caught the scent of a pheasant or quail or we could have lost him, as Paul didn't have the whistle that called him "home" with him. When Stratoliner caught that scent, he forsook all the basics of life to follow his instinct.

Stratoliner was a problem at first because he was a "running" dog. That is one who covers ground by the mile rather than by the acre. I couldn't attend the very first trial I had him entered in, but I called Paul the evening after he was scheduled to compete. "How did he make out?"

"Wasn't judged."

Huh? My inner translator failed. "What do you mean, he wasn't judged? Why not? Did he get sick?"

"No. Lost."

"WHAT!?!?"

Paul picked up on my panic and virtually spewed out words. "Sheriff's looking for him. Everybody's looking."

I managed to draw the story out, a word at a time. Stratoliner had made such a huge cast that he had ended up clear out of the county. Well, someone thought there was a sighting in the next county, anyway.

After putting so much money into the dream of having a top bird dog, it was unthinkable that I might lose him without ever even seeing him in a single trial. I sat beside my wife on the sofa and imagined all the things that could happen to him, alone and loose, none of them good. And with me in Pennsylvania and him in South Carolina, there was nothing I could do except worry.

So that's what I did—for three hours until Paul called back. "Sheriff found your dog."

"Is he okay? Where was he? What was he doing?"

I could hear Paul's shrug over the phone. "Pointing."

It took a while, but Stratoliner caught on to what we wanted him to do. He remained what they call a "big running dog," making initial casts so big he appeared the smallest white speck on the horizon. This was flashy and very eye-catching for the judges, but he was always hard to control, and my heart was always in my throat until he responded to a call from Paul or me.

One of my proudest moments occurred at the English Setter Club's 50th Anniversary Amateur Trial, held in Medford, New Jersey. In honor of the occasion, the club's logo, a setter on point, was cast in solid gold and affixed to the sterling silver trays instead of the usual solid sterling silver logo. The turnout was impressive, the competition fierce. All the amateur owners, including me, longed for a trophy.

Edward J.
Scanlon

This trial was unusual because there were no birds occurring naturally in the field. Instead, quail were planted in a hedgerow, where the gallery could have a good view, for the dogs to find. New birds were planted after each brace, to give all the dogs a fair chance to show their capability.

In our case, my challenge was to get Stratoliner to the bird field before the half-hour was up. His cast was so wide that getting him to come in to the hedgerow field, which was very close to the gallery, in just a half-hour was going to require all my skill. That dog liked to run. If he was late to the bird field, he would be disqualified, no questions asked or excuses given. To add to the tension, we had drawn The Builder as a brace mate. Stratoliner had a slightly better competition record than his pricier brother, but The Builder was no slouch.

When I released the dog, my worries about keeping him in the area proved valid. He cast to the very edge of the small farm, almost out of sight, and he refused to respond to my first whistle. He was having too much fun, going boldly where no dog had gone before.

I repeated my whistle, with some trepidation. Stratoliner knew from the few other events I had handled him in that (unlike Paul Walker, for whom he would respond quickly) I was no pro. When he finally started to come in, I realized I had only five minutes to get him on the birds. That would give him barely enough time to show one point, much less the two or three that some of the other dogs had done.

After a few more minutes of whistling my head off, we finally reached the field. I saw the judge consult his watch. "Two minutes," he warned me.

When Stratoliner finally struck his beautiful, rigid point, with less than a minute and a half to spare, I dismounted, trying to make it look as if I had planned this moment of tension. The gallery was on the edge of its seats, wondering if I would make the flush and shot in time.

Unfortunately, I was so nervous I put the gun barrel in my mouth instead of the whistle.

"For God's sake, get that gun out of your mouth, flush the damn bird, and shoot. You've got thirty seconds!" the judge said, caught between a laugh and exasperation. I suspect the time really was up, but the judge was tolerant and gave us our chance. I flushed the bird and fired, Stratoliner all the while remaining steady as one of the gold dogs on the trophies.

"Time," the judge called.

I retired from the field to receive Paul's assessment, succinct as always. "Cast, hunt, good. Time, numbers, bad." Paul felt Stratoliner had made the best casts of any of the dogs and was the best at the hunt. His point was perfect, but I had barely made the field in time and had only one point. It all would depend on how much the judges counted the time and the single find.

I was all nerves for the three hours until the decisions were announced. I wondered how the owners whose dogs had gone the first day stood the waiting. I told myself that even if we didn't make the top three, as we had to do to win a trophy, we had done well. There were close to forty entries, a lot of them darn good.

I don't remember who won first and second anymore, but I sure remember who won third, because we did. The superior casts and point had made up for the time and the single find.

That night I returned to the hotel in triumph. I was so happy I didn't mind the other competitors' good-natured ribbing about how I had so despaired of Stratoliner's performance that I tried to end it all, right on the field.

Another high point was when Paul Walker handled my pride and joy to a win in the National Pheasant Championship at Baldwinsville, New York, in the late '50s. Stratoliner won the trial and yet was not awarded the title Champion. The judges had the discretion to withhold the title Champion if in their judgment the winner's performance was not worthy of that coveted title. So, after a weeklong trial and giving the best performance of the many dogs entered, Stratoliner was a winner but still not a champion. It was a bitter pill. I questioned the judges, as I thought Stratoliner's work was perfect. The older judge cautioned me, "Doc, don't become what we call 'kennel blind.' We fall in love with our dogs and can see no faults. Recall, he let down hunting the last ten minutes and lacked a true champion's finish." He was right. My reluctance to accept his judgment didn't change the facts.

Stratoliner finally acquired the title Champion in Canada when he won the so-called Chicken Championship the next year. Unfortunately, I was too busy to attend but read and rejoiced over the published description of the feat in *Field and Stream* magazine. Paul even gave me a stride-by-stride and point-by-point description (but only after considerable badgering). He was equally proud, and his purse was considerable.

A few final words about the top professional field trial trainers and handlers of that time. Theirs was a labor of pure love. They received a modest monthly fee per dog and all the prize money. For this, they trained and handled their charges all over the country, driving thousands of miles in their dog trucks, and of course they also had to truck their horses and pay their assistants. There wasn't one I know of who couldn't have made far more money in another job with less hours and less effort. Paul Walker explained it in his usual few words: "Field trial dogs are a chronic disease. Can't get rid of it. It's an addiction."

Stratoliner and most of his littermates from the incestuous mating of Fast Delivery and Delivery Boy's Girl died relatively young. Stratoliner's brother, The Builder, was dead at five years. Stratoliner had to be put down at only five and half years of age. A fungal lung infection was his downfall. His loss was very painful to me. My feeling is that the inbreeding somehow hurt their immune systems' ability to fight off the disease invaders that attack all dogs. It shortened their lives!

After my Stratoliner's demise, I continued for a year or two with Helicopter, one of his sons, a nice dog but just not a winner. The pressures of what had become a huge, four-veterinarian practice permitted my attendance at only a few major trials a year. I gradually gave up my participation, but not my interest in or love of the sport. I still treasure the memories of beautiful fall days, astride a good horse, watching Stratoliner frozen on point, steady as a rock as the bird winged away and the gun shot.

Thankfully, such great memories can still be revisited often. Today, field trials are an almost defunct sport. Trials require a lot of open fields and territory unspoiled by pollution. Urban sprawl has contributed to the decline of this sport. I was fortunate to have enjoyed it during its heyday.

eight

Picasso, the Dog They Couldn't Kill

Passing through my waiting room, headed for an examination, I stopped and stared impolitely at her. Mrs. Walsh and a few waiting clients, equally impolite, were also gawking. Maybe excusable? After all, how many women wore a full-length, flowing cloak in the early morning, especially one of a glowing, satin-like royal purple? Her dress was a blinding bright red, her shoes the highest-heeled patent leather. The long, dark hair, the large hoop earrings, the huge golden necklace somehow spelled Gypsy.

It turned out she was Violetta DeMazia, famous in the world of fine art as a teacher, an author, and a director of the fabulous Barnes Foundation fine arts museum in nearby Merion. A striking and impressive figure, she used her arms, hands, and body in a theatrical manner. Her voice was in the low, measured tones of an experienced lecturer. Yes, she was an aristocratic, handsome eye-catcher and well aware of the impression she made. Certainly an atypical Main Liner; no mink coats or tennis shoes for her.

According to my secretary-detective, Violetta was more than a foundation director, teacher, and art advisor to the wealthy Dr. Barnes. She was also "you know what" to him. The term *mistress* was too indelicate for Mrs. Walsh. "Of course, you know how the Main Line gossips," she whispered. I did indeed.

Violetta's choice of pets, a miniature Italian greyhound named Picasso, was, in the canine sense, equally elegant and impressive. He was fine-boned, chiseled, and fragile-looking. At first glance, one's impression was that a strong wind would carry him away like Toto in *The Wizard of Oz*, but looks can be deceiving. He was nearly indestructible, as I learned on three occasions.

Picasso was first presented to me as a three-month-old pup. He grew nicely, with no health problems. Personality-wise, he was aloof and dignified but not unfriendly. Like his owner, he made a statement even when he sat still. However, he had one character defect that caused a long hospitalization stay when he was about fourteen months old.

I learned that he was an "escape artist." If anyone left the front door open, he would take off. The back door led to a walled garden, so no escape was possible there. The little guy was determined to escape and see the world, though, and was creative in his efforts to run. Violetta rationalized his bad habit as a desire to hunt. Unlike its large relatives, grey-hounds and whippets, though, Picasso's breed is usually considered more ornamental and companionable.

Violetta dearly loved her companion and took every precaution to prevent his escape. "Where there is a will, there is a way" could have been written for our little Houdini. One day when he escaped, he met the irresistible force in the form of a large refuse collection truck, and the results were nearly disastrous. He was a pathetic sight. Stretched out on the exam table on a white blanket that appeared to hold more blood than his body did, he was in deep shock. The massive bleeding, the pale oral mucous membranes spelled a dreadful prognosis. It was obvious without X-rays or palpation that the distorted front legs were broken. He was unconscious. Skull injuries? Very likely, with the large, gaping wound above his eyes. His very shallow, irregular respirations were also ominous. It looked like Houdini was about to perform his final escape act. I was disheartened. I had buried too many like him.

Violetta, though trembling and distraught, showed her breeding in her admirable control. "Is there any chance he can be saved?" she asked quietly.

I thought he would last at best a half-hour, the damage was so massive. "Please go home," I told her. "I have to get to work on him immediately. I'll call you. There's always a chance while he's alive." Her sense of dignity was as great as her little dog's, but at that moment she looked so forlorn I did something one shouldn't do to a woman client (very elderly women excepted)—I hugged her. "Go home, Ms. DeMazia, I'll call."

To everyone's amazement, especially mine, after blood typing and a transfusion from one of our resident donors, Picasso responded within nine hours. There was still a serious concussion and the multiple fractures to contend with, but he was alive. Within the next twenty-four hours, his vital signs were almost stable. Hallelujah!

Picasso was lucky again. While I had confidence in my ability to handle ordinary fractures, Picasso needed the best. Although mostly retired and a busy traveler, Dr. Stader was at home. The master orthopedic surgeon was excited. Two shattered foreleg bones, a fractured pelvis, a dislocated rear leg plus a broken femur would give him hours of surgical pleasure—and such tiny bones to work on! He rubbed his hands with anticipation. I had wanted only the best for Picasso, and the Great One provided it in spades. The long, involved surgery was everything Dr. Stader hoped it would be—challenging—and everything I hoped it would be—successful.

After two and a half months of hospitalization, the escape artist returned home, ready to "hunt" another day. "Do you think he learned his lesson about running away?" questioned Violetta.

"Don't count on it." I brushed his healthy, burnished coat. "The probability is he has no recollections. He never knew what hit him." Picasso knew we were talking about him; he turned his head and pushed his muzzle into my hand. I had grown quite fond of him in our ten weeks together. He was courageous and spirited, and a very handsome fellow.

Picasso's life went along uneventfully for more than a year. I did counsel Violetta to curtail the food treats, though, as he was becoming overweight. She entertained world-famous artists, collectors, and the social elite. I could visualize the Russian caviar on little crackers, the goose liver pâté tidbits his begging brown eyes would earn. She was a caring, sensible owner, though, and followed my advice. He lost the extra blubber.

Picasso's second brush with death occurred about a year after the dreadful truck accident. To understand some possible reasons for the incident, a little background on the Barnes Foundation museum is helpful. Dr. Barnes's huge fortune was the result of his discovery of a silver-based antiseptic ointment called Argyrol, and he had three factories here and abroad. Long before our present medical miracles, it was, so to speak, the only skin treatment in town. It was also used to treat venereal diseases, and they were rampant. There was no penicillin available at the time. It may not have been very effective, but it was the basis of his fortune.

Barnes was a unique thinker, with vast ideas and knowledge. He had great compassion for the "average working man," and he began educational discussion groups among his workers. He hung his treasured paintings in the factories for all to share, study, and discuss. This became so popular that he eventually held additional sessions to include people from outside his company. But his respect for the common man made him unpopular, as he felt there should be full equality for blacks and he worked for civil rights in an era when there was no such thing. He believed an educated society is the key to democracy.

To build his art collection, Barnes and Violetta made annual forays to Europe and elsewhere to acquire the treasures. He had "the eye," an uncanny ability to spot the young and future great artists. He also had money to buy the already recognized ones, and he included in his collection almost every important artist.

The result was probably the largest and rarest private art collection in the world. His incomparable collection of Cézannes has traveled the world and been exhibited at major cities to large, appreciative audiences. The value, number, and diversity of his holdings eclipsed those of such renowned collectors as Walter Annenberg. He erected a gem of a building to house his treasures on his Merion estate, not too far from my hospital. He permitted only a few people at a time to view the collection, and visiting hours were very restrictive. Essentially, he controlled who was allowed access, and when. People often waited months for a tour, and most were turned away.

The doctor had a distaste for inherited privilege, as he was a self-made man. He certainly offended some of the Philadelphia "high and mighty." The foundation was always at war with its wealthy neighbors. Barnes also incurred the wrath of the *Philadelphia Inquirer,* the city's premier newspaper. The *Inquirer* contended that since the foundation was tax exempt, it should truly be open to the public. Reporters wrote many scathing articles about Dr. Barnes and about the director. They pooh-poohed Violetta's daily art classes and teaching as a "pretense" to limit and exclude visitors. The foundation, they said, was a toy and a hobby for a wealthy, eccentric man—not something that should accrue the benefits of a tax-exempt status. (Barnes's actions belied the paper's words, however. When he died in 1951 in an auto accident, he left the stewardship of the foundation to Lincoln University, the first African-American college.)

Dr. Barnes and Violetta remained steadfast in their visitors policy. For certain, they had made enemies. The doctor was considered very arrogant and Violetta, while kind and friendly to those close to her, gave the appearance of aloofness. They, of course, became embittered by the media and refused any interviews. Even the wiliest incognito reporters couldn't con them into a comment, much less an interview.

Picasso's second life-threatening episode was definitely the result of a cowardly, malicious enemy. He was the victim of strychnine poisoning. The poison was disguised in a beef filet bait thrown over the garden wall. Several such baits were found by a detective. Little Picasso's greed for treats made it a sure thing he would fall victim. Violetta's immediate neighbors were exonerated; she led a quiet life and was well liked.

Fortunately, Violetta saw Picasso's first violent convulsions, just as he returned from his morning toilet. Also lucky was the fact that I was at the hospital at 7:30 in the morning instead of my usual 7:45. From my SPCA experience, I was unhappily familiar with the symptoms, having seen and treated many strychnine poisoning cases. In the congested city neighborhoods, it was at one time the poison of choice to kill the pet of a feuding neighbor. Later, rat poison, warfarin, became available in all hardware stores, and it became the number-one choice for the pet assassins.

Strychnine produces dreadful convulsions with stiff, extended, sawhorse-like limbs. Picasso's head and neck were extended in a locked-jaw fashion. I quickly filled a syringe with the pentobarbital antidote, found his tiny vein on the first try, and slowly injected the life-saving fluid while praying, praying. The convulsions subsided. The danger now was to balance the dosage; the antidote itself was deadly. I had to give just enough to control the convulsions. He was such a small dog; it was difficult to judge the dosage, especially under such pressure. I did have a deep affection for the rascal and could feel my sweat as I mentally prayed.

Again, Picasso's luck held. He was indeed a survivor. If

Violetta had presented him just five minutes later, the outcome would have been death. I kept him for the day, just in case, even though we had emptied his stomach. He was one wrung-out dog for twenty-four hours afterward, doing nothing but sleeping, but no serious or lingering damage had occurred. I remember thinking at the time that this dog was charmed. I thought that if someone pointed a loaded gun at his head and pulled the trigger, the gun would misfire. It seemed Picasso would die only of old, old age.

Through house calls and Picasso's two near-death experiences, Violetta and I had become comfortable with each other. She thought I could medically "walk on water." Not only were my fees paid on time and in full, but I also received a case of fine French champagne and a note of thanks. She was truly grateful to me.

This gave me the courage to make a personal request. Knowing the policy of "no interviews," I was prepared for a refusal. Daughter number three, Patricia, was a senior in high school and her English assignment was to interview an imaginary or real person on a subject of interest. Violetta agreed to do an interview with the caveat that she might not answer certain questions.

A date for the interview, to include high tea, was scheduled at Violetta's home. Pat was, of course, thrilled at the prospect of viewing Violetta's not inconsiderable personal art collection. I have always been grateful to Violetta for the way she treated my daughter that day. Pat still talks about her as charming, stunningly dressed, and most cordial. Pat received an A in English, to our mutual pleasure, and for quite a while after wore bright purple.

Picasso gave his owner another fright. Although a dog with angio-neurotic edema is a scary sight, the condition is rarely fatal. The victim's appearance is the source of the old expression "swelled up like a piz'ned pup." The body can be covered with hive-like swellings and the head and facial tissues grotesquely bloated. It is the result of an allergic reaction, often from bee stings. Violetta's walled-in garden was large, planted with a riotous display of flowers, and naturally inhabited by many pollinators. Picasso resented them and attacked with gusto. I found several in his oral cavity.

His head, face, lips, and eyelids were grossly swollen, his eyes barely visible. Violetta was near panic and tears when she begged, "After all he's been through, we can't lose him now, can we?" This type of case is, in a sense, a vet's dream. The doctor is almost certain to have a normal, healthy patient within an hour or two, as well as a very grateful owner. The antidote, an antihistamine, is almost 100 percent effective.

"Everything will be all right," I assured her, directing her to my private office. Mrs. Walsh offered her the usual glass of cold water (why do we do that?) and also reassured her. In about forty-five minutes, Picasso was returning to a recognizable state and within hours, he was on his way home. Picasso was again a survivor, and I was the medical hero.

Again, I took advantage of his grateful owner, and secured a private viewing of the art treasures at the Barnes Foundation museum for my wife and myself. All the publicity had aroused my curiosity, and my wife was an admirer of fine art.

It was a wonderful day. Viewing room after room of the world's great works of art in absolute quiet, no rustling of catalogues, no whispers of fellow visitors, was almost a religious experience. I had by then seen the Louvre, the Prado, and many excellent museums in Europe and America, but the Barnes collection was, to me, better than its billing. I was truly awestruck—an unforgettable experience.

Violetta's private art collection fetched over $30 million upon the liquidation of her estate. Picasso, predictably, died in his sleep an old, old dog, a year before his mistress's demise. Years later, my daughter Martha had an Italian greyhound, and I could never see him without thinking about the elegant Violetta, and Picasso, the dog they couldn't kill.

A final art story. Without apology, I will state that I am one of the few people who have desecrated great paintings by a world-famous artist with impunity, and on several occasions.

The famous Philadelphia sculptor Samuel Murray was a great-uncle to me through marriage. He is best known for his statue of Commodore Barry (father of the American navy) in Fairmount Park, the Boise Penrose statue in the state capitol in Harrisburg, and his work on *Winged Victory*, the Pennsylvania state monument at the Gettysburg Battlefield. He sculpted many busts for prominent and wealthy Main Liners of that era.

Uncle Sam was also an instructor in sculpture at the Pennsylvania Academy of the Fine Arts in Philadelphia. His colleague and close friend, Thomas Eakins, was an instructor in painting. They made headlines together in their time, picketing the academy because they were not permitted to use live nude models in their classes. They won their cause. It is hard to believe it was once a cause célèbre, garnering many media headlines.

They had exchanged gifts of their works over the years. Uncle Sam's spacious studio was jammed with sculptures, and he was forced to store many of the famous painter's gifts of oil paintings in the large, closet-like toilet room at the back of his studio. The family often visited Uncle Sam on Sunday afternoons, and we were served tea and cookies. Being very young, I waited till the last moment to answer the tea's diuretic action. In haste, and failing to be able to find or reach the string to light the only bulb in the toilet room, my aim was often amiss. Millions of dollars' worth of Eakins's works were inadvertently decorated with my distended bladder's issue. Simply put, I peed on them.

I'm not proud of it, but on occasion, the story has been valuable. Its recitation silenced several boring, self-appointed art experts. At worst, it caused a change of subject.

Youth is often thoughtless and unappreciative. It was many years before I understood and appreciated the greatness of the art produced by Uncle Sam and his colleague Thomas Eakins.

nine

Upstairs, Downstairs

Are you a little awed in the presence of famous or very rich people? I was quite a bit as a young man, and I suspect I had lots of company. Maybe it's my Irish peasant roots. I'll relate an occasion, however, when I was unawed, in complete control, and very comfortable in such a presence.

It was a lovely, warm summer evening and I arrived a few minutes late for my usual 7 to 8 evening office hours. There were two cars parked in front of my clinic. One was a station wagon belonging to a client scheduled to pick up some worm medications. The other was an unimpressive, older Ford sedan.

It took only a minute to dispense the medicine and I turned my attention to an elderly woman and a barrel-chested, dark-haired man around fifty, with a Kerry blue terrier on a leash. I had no recollection of seeing the Kerry before, and I thought, *Good! A new client!* You don't see many Kerries anymore, which is a shame. They are good pets, cheerful, non-shedding, although somewhat demanding with their energy.

We went to the examining room, where I filled out a patient card. The lady, in a slight foreign accent, offered the usual information. At this point I assumed they were mother and son. Meanwhile, the Kerry had dribbled a little urine on the floor (not uncommon with a nervous dog). The man quickly took a paper towel, erased the liquid, and threw the towel in my refuse container.

The gentleman, dressed in rumpled khaki slacks and a white button-down, short-sleeved summer shirt, related that the dog had been ill for only two days. As he spoke, I detected a very slight lisp in his measured speech. I examined the dog and determined that we were dealing with an upper respiratory infection, which could be an early symptom of our old enemy, distemper. I gave him the good news that it was a mild case and since the dog was fully grown and in good condition, the prognosis was good.

"Now," I quickly glanced at the patient card for the owner's name, "Mr. Annenberg, if it is distemper it is highly contagious, so keep him away from the neighborhood dogs."

"I have three other dogs at home," he said.

"Have they shown any symptoms?"

He glanced at his companion. She replied, "Nein."

"Good. We have a serum that might well abort the virus. It should be given immediately, so I suggest you bring them in right away."

"That will be a little difficult with three of them. Do you make house calls?"

Mindful of the old Ford outside, I answered, "Yes, but it will cost you more than if I administered the serum here."

He paused, gave me an odd look, and said, "That will be all right. Why don't you follow me home? I live nearby."

Since I had no other clients waiting, I agreed. "Give me a few minutes to get the serum and syringes." I filled my black bag, which I was pleased to note was beginning to look used, got in my car, and followed.

He turned on Cherry Lane, a street noted for its magnificent homes and estates. I looked around, marveling at how beautiful it all was, in no way able to guess that in five years I would be able to move my family one street over. I speculated: Maybe they lived in a servant's home and worked for a wealthy family. No, that didn't make sense. Servants were unlikely to be permitted four pets.

As we turned into a long, tree-lined drive, with several sand-trapped golf holes on one side, and approached a beautiful stone mansion, the light dawned. Annenberg—good grief! He was Walter Annenberg, publisher of the *Philadelphia Inquirer,* the *Daily Racing Form* (a huge cash cow), and many other publications. The old Ford, it turned out, belonged to the cook.

I remember reading once that Sam Walton, owner of the Wal-Mart chain, was the wealthiest man in America. (This was pre–Bill Gates America.) Never, though, did I hear of Walton's giving $50 million to $100 million to a charity, year in and year out, as did the Annenberg Foundation. This, to me, made this man larger than life.

My usual awe began to set in, accentuated by acute embarrassment at not recognizing him and suggesting he save money by bringing his dogs to the clinic. It was quickly alleviated, though, by my short-sleeved, courteous, smiling host. "Dr. Scanlon, anything you need, please ask. I called my gardener John to assist you." John, small in stature, with a handlebar mustache, was perfect. His strong, weather-beaten, callused hands were gentle but firm. He held the dogs still as I injected the serum.

When I had finished, John advised, "Mr. Annenberg would like to see you in the house. He wants to know about after-care and further treatment."

I followed him from the large, well-designed kennel to the mansion house called Innwood, where our future ambassador to England met me in the foyer. "Come in, Dr. Scanlon. Any problems?"

"No, your gardener was a big help. Now, about the after-care . . ."

He interrupted, "Let's go in the library and you can write down your instructions. I'll see they are followed. I have to leave for California in the morning, but I have reliable people." I later found out how well he treated them. No wonder they were reliable.

"Now, Dr. Scanlon, I'm frequently away so I'm leaving instructions that any future veterinary care needed for our dogs and cats is to be entrusted to you. Submit your fees to my personal attention, and my manager will pay them."

"I appreciate that very much, Mr. Annenberg." What an understatement!

He went on, "We like your weekly column on pet care in the *Inquirer* very much. I read it every Sunday."

So that was the reason I had acquired my famous, rich new client. I had momentarily forgotten that his paper carried my column, which answered letters sent in by pet owners. It also never occurred to me that the owner and publisher read such minor pieces, and my only contact at the paper was with the editor. At that time, the column earned $60 a week, a very welcome addition to my practice income.

"Sometime in the future we'll have to discuss it. I have some ideas," the publisher said. I wondered what he meant, but soon forgot the remark.

That was the last time I saw Mr. Annenberg for many years. John, the gardener, dutifully brought in the pets for care and semiannual checkups, and he and I came to enjoy each other's company. Over the years, he was the source of many Annenberg stories (he was quite a talker, and at times difficult to get rid of). Since he didn't pay my fees, some of the visits were unnecessary, or borderline.

It was apparent how much John thought of his employer, and he sometimes voiced his concern for him: "You know, Doc, even billionaires' lives aren't all roses. Mr. Annenberg's only son committed suicide while he was a student in college.

He took that awful hard—never did seem to get over it. His only daughter had some emotional problems also. Did you know he has a malformed ear and is deaf on one side?"

One time I remarked on his employer's famous philanthropy, as he had recently provided the multimillion-dollar Annenberg School of Communications to my alma mater, the University of Pennsylvania. "Doc, there may be more to it than you know." He lowered his voice conspiratorially. "His father, old Moses, was sick and released from jail to die at home. He was serving time for tax evasion and some other white-collar stuff. Now, Walter was his only son, and Moses asked him to clean up the Annenberg name so it wasn't equated with anything dirty or illegal. It wasn't easy. People don't realize when Mr. A took over the *Inquirer,* he also assumed over ten million dollars in debt in back taxes owed by his father's estate."

"Well," I said as I completed the cat's exam, "he certainly filled his father's request in spades. I can't think of a businessman who has a better reputation or is more charitable."

"Besides that," John continued, "he's generous by nature. We, all the servants, eat the same food the family does, not like some bosses who pinch every penny." He tweaked his mustache, which over the years had grown to be a true compulsive gesture. "Believe me, his seven sisters are all millionaires because of Mr. A's capabilities and generosity. He was left in total control of the business by his father and could have easily cut the women out."

Occasionally I received a clipping from a newspaper or magazine regarding a new drug or procedure. There would be a notation: "Interesting?" or "Have you seen this?" It was initialed by Walter and wrapped in his personal stationery. How a man with his huge responsibilities could take the time for gestures like that was beyond me. Maybe that was one reason he was so successful—he kept abreast of details and understood the importance of kind gestures.

I made one of the biggest financial mistakes of my life with my *Inquirer* pet care column. My practice had eventually flourished to the point where there weren't enough hours in the day, and as I tried to figure out how to find more time, I thought I could forgo the $60 from my writing. I wrote a letter to my editor, advising that the enclosed two columns were the last I could supply. I thanked him for his help in editing and for his encouragement. The paper had a new veterinary writer quickly, and never missed an issue.

Now, how did I miss out on a junior-sized fortune? Here's the story: I ran into my editor a few months later at a local restaurant. "You know, Doc, I'll never understand your giving up your column." I explained how busy I was, a growing family and a possible second hospital planned. "Did you know Mr. Annenberg had planned to talk to you about syndication? He wanted you to get a little more seasoning first and then he was going to put you in touch with the best. He was planning to set it up for you. You might have ended up being published in fifty or sixty papers."

I was stunned. If the *Inquirer* paid $60 for one weekly column, what would fifty columns generate? Even at $40, it would bring in about $2,000 per week, or $104,000 per year! What had I done? I'm sure I was a little pale and bilious-looking when I asked, "Is it too late to get back in?"

He smiled. "You only get one bite of the apple in publishing, Ed. Have you noticed your replacement is doing as well as, maybe better than, you were? We're getting more letters." Understandable. I had given the column less and less attention in the last few months. Syndication had never crossed my mind.

I couldn't even say good-bye. I was just thankful I didn't regurgitate. What a dummy! If handled properly, I might have become the Ann Landers of veterinary-care fame, and very wealthy. I believe that Mr. Annenberg would have called me if he had been aware of my resignation. He was away, tending his far-flung empire. My loss.

Over the years, Walter's fortune grew, as did his philanthropy. One year, he gave away $500 million for education. Another year he gave his great art collection, for which he had been offered $1 billion, to New York's Metropolitan Museum of Art. In 1999, he was called the greatest living philanthropist.

The second and final time I saw Mr. Annenberg was in London. At that time, he was our ambassador to the Court of Saint James's, our highest representative in England. I had called for an appointment for my wife and me to visit, hoping to be part of a group tour of the newly refurbished embassy. Mr. Annenberg had had it redecorated, at his personal expense, to the tune of $2 million.

To my surprise, he sent a limousine to our hotel. Ever mindful of detail, he had seen my request to visit. We were transported to and from our hotel and given a personal tour by Mr. Ambassador himself. My wife couldn't believe we were given the same treatment as royalty or international diplomats. "He's so warm and friendly. He's just like us," she exclaimed. "Yeah," I laughed. "Give or take a few billion." It was the highlight of our European tour.

My girls also experienced the Annenberg gestures of kindness. When we had moved to that area, the girls would insist the Annenberg mansion be first on their Halloween trick-or-treat route. They were always greeted at the door by a butler in full uniform, including white gloves, who would with great seriousness and dignity praise their costumes as he presented them with an abundance of delicacies, insisting they choose several. "Daddy," they would tease me, mouths full of petits fours or nougat, "when are we going to get a butler, and what about getting those nice sand traps on our lawn?"

How lucky I was to have met such a great man and cared for his animals. I often think of his kindness and common touch. In many ways, he was indeed "just like us." Great wealth doesn't always spoil one.

Although in the area where my practice was located there were many wealthy people, there were also pockets of poverty and low-income housing, so I had many pet owners with modest incomes. They, too, loved their animals and despite the strain on their budgets, for the most part paid their bills. Some paid a little each month, but they were faithful. In those days, we didn't charge interest on unpaid balances.

There was one widow who remains in clear focus in my memory, a Mrs. Rososki, whom I admired. She had lost her husband about a year before I first administered to their new sheltie pup. Mrs. Walsh had furnished the information that she lived in a very small row house (this was before row houses became fashionable and were transformed into "townhouses") and cared for her wheelchair-bound, invalid father. My secretary-detective also knew she had a part-time job that offered no pension or Social Security. She was chronically short of funds. As the years had progressed, my office call fees had gradually grown from two dollars to ten. Mindful of her situation, I had noted on her card that she was to be charged only three dollars. Somehow, when a new card was added to her large file, the notation was lost.

One day we had our usual pleasant annual visit. Her sheltie, a particularly beautiful, now aging bitch called Tri-Sox, had the cheerful, perky disposition so typical of the breed. I gave her a thorough exam and an anti-rabies vaccine. I enjoyed Mrs. Rososki, and always found her disposition to be like her dog's—cheerful, positive, upbeat, and humorous.

I passed the record card to my substitute secretary (Mrs. Walsh being out on a sick day), who, not knowing our special treatment of this client, presented Mrs. Rososki with a bill for $14, $10 for the office visit and $4 for the vaccine.

The waiting room was jammed full of people, dogs, and cats when Mrs. Rososki loudly denounced me to everyone as a robber, a thief, and an unscrupulous money-grubber. Her normally sweet, modulated voice became unbelievably loud and harsh. She not only refused to pay, but concluded her tirade by declaring she would be finding a new vet. Everyone in the waiting room was staring in stunned silence. I cringed with embarrassment.

When Mrs. Walsh, the diplomat, came back the next day, she called Mrs. Rososki and explained that, unbeknownst to her, she had been given special fees for years, and that I would be truly saddened if not permitted to continue to care for her dog. She did come back at the three-dollar fee, but we never again had the easy relationship we had had before her verbal castigation. Did you ever hear the expression "No good deed goes unpunished"?

My patients were mostly medically challenging and always interesting. The two-legged animals on the other end of the leash were sometimes dull and boring and occasionally considered the pet a trial, a headache. These owners had frequently inherited or were forced to live with the pet through marriage, sort of animal-world stepchildren. Sometimes they actually resented the pet or even hated it.

One such owner was Mrs. Oliver Brittingham. She was the second wife, and along with her rotund, jolly Oliver, she had acquired his unusual pet, an ocelot. He dearly loved India, and fussed over and pampered her. She always wore one of several heavily bejeweled collars. India was troubled by an occasional flare-up of otitis, or inflammation of the external ear canal. This necessitated daily treatment for two or three days. Oliver refused to leave her in the hospital for treatment, which suited me. He insisted his wife bring her in for treatment when he was not available. "I don't want my darling pussums in a nasty hospital," he proclaimed behind his wife's disgusted look.

"My old lady," as he fondly called Mrs. B., made no bones about her dislike of "pussums" on the occasions she brought the ocelot in without Oliver. "She is a pain in the you-know-what. Spoiled, ungrateful, she couldn't care less about Oliver." Was she talking about the cat or herself? "He makes a fool of himself over her. I wish she would run away, get lost or killed," she sneered on one visit.

Well, the time came when it looked like Mrs. B. just might get her wish. "Pussums" was brought in with a mild upper respiratory infection. It didn't respond to treatment, and progressed to her lungs. She also had no appetite, always a danger sign. "Now, Mr. Brittingham," I advised, "this is serious. India needs twice-daily antibiotic injections, IV fluid therapy, lab work, and constant monitoring. I know you don't want her hospitalized, but she can't be treated properly at home. I'll need to isolate her. She'll be kept away from my other patients."

India, minus her jewelry and ensconced in the "private room," responded some after twenty-four hours, but her lungs sounded terrible the following day. Pneumonia, no question. She was running a high, intractable fever, so her prognosis was poor.

"Mrs. Brittingham is out front," Mrs. Walsh announced, "and she wants to talk to you privately." A question crossed my mind. Had she had a change of heart? Was she really concerned about India?

No. I knew venom when I heard and saw it. The gist of our conversation was amazing. It was the first and last time I was ever solicited to be a "hit man" to a pet. She was blunt about it. "Doctor, if India dies in your hospital, I will really make it worth your while." I was struck dumb. Tongue-tied. She must have taken my silence for consideration. "Name a figure. It will be cash." My tongue was still lost. She continued, "Oliver would kill me, so you know no one would ever find out from me or you."

Speech returned. Equally bluntly, I retorted, "Mrs. Brittingham, that is the most insulting, disgusting offer I've ever had. You are also disgusting. Please leave."

As she headed for the closed door, she stopped and paid me a compliment: "I was afraid of your stupid reaction. I've always thought you were one of those goody-goody types."

India, despite everything I could do, including a consultation with the vet in charge of cats at the Philadelphia Zoo, died. Mrs. B. only thought she had won, though.

Oliver took her body to a taxidermist, who did a masterful

job. "Pussums," 100 percent lifelike, was placed, complete with one of her jeweled collars, in a tree in his large foyer. She looked down on all visitors and family, her mouth partly open, the white fangs visible. Although declawed, her large forearm was extended, and had been fitted with fake claws. Oliver insisted I visit and see her, and I couldn't get out of it gracefully. "Isn't she beautiful? I can even hear her purr," he smiled. I was certain that, as she entered and left the house daily, Mrs. B. could also hear her purr.

Leading me to the door, Oliver whispered, "Don't say anything to my old lady. I know I can never replace my pussums, but I am looking for a new cub. I want it to be a surprise!" Leaving, I mentally wished him luck with a new pet. He certainly deserved something in his life besides Mrs. B.

ten

Deadbeats

Every business, every professional encounters the deadbeats. These are the people who are unwilling to pay their bills and plan to steal from you from the word "go," as opposed to those unfortunate people who occasionally find themselves unable to pay their debts. The interesting thing, from my experience, is the ends to which the deadbeats will go, the time, the efforts, and the deceptions they devise in order to avoid payment. If their energies were directed toward honest endeavor, they could be astonishingly successful.

Deadbeats come in all forms, from all professions and income levels. I've had a famous movie star, a very prominent lawyer, entertainers, and Six-Pack Joes beat me out of my fees. I found it best to just write them off because no way, in most cases, could I best them and collect. They were just too good at the avoidance game for me to compete. Some of their machinations were almost admirable, in the sense that they were so clever.

A young man, Terrence T. Tobias (I should have been suspicious of the name, but that's what his parents supposedly
named him), came in, accompanied by a good-looking German shepherd with a salivary cyst. He related the history. The
cyst had been operated on by another vet, with no results. The
cyst had reappeared beneath the lower jaws, and it was hanging in a very unsightly manner. Tobias had heard of my skills
(flattery) and felt if anyone could correct the problem,
I could.

He claimed he wasn't concerned with the cost and produced a check indicating he was willing to pay in advance. I
subsequently learned that not caring about the cost was often
a tip-off that a person was a deadbeat. It was a Thursday, and
since Tobias would pick the dog up Saturday after a Friday
surgery, the check wouldn't have time to clear. At that time, I
wasn't thinking of the clearance mechanics but was, of
course, impressed by his willingness to pay in advance. We
agreed he would pay upon the pet's discharge because I didn't
know what the final drug charges would be. The surgery went
well and I felt confident the entire cyst had been removed. If
any part of the cyst were not removed, it would recur, which
had happened with the first surgery.

On Saturday, the expert con man cheerfully signed a check
imprinted with his name and address. It was drawn on a big
Philadelphia bank and, surprise, it was soon returned with the
notation that the account had been closed. Tobias wasn't
listed in the Philadelphia phone book. Well, I reasoned, he
might be in a job where it was best to have an unlisted home
number. At that time, unlisted numbers were scarce, but not
unheard of.

Recollecting his clean-cut looks and dress and his eye-to-
eye conversation, I hoped there had been an honest mistake.
After all, writing a check on a closed account was a criminal
offense. Maybe, I tried to convince myself, he had mistakenly
used an old check. The bill was sizable. The surgery was delicate and time-consuming. I wanted my fee and I especially

wanted Tobias, because the more I thought about it, the more I was sure I'd been deceived.

The address on his check was a well-known street in North Philadelphia. It happened that one of my kennel men resided in the area. I gave him a five-dollar bill, explained the situation, and asked him to make an evening collection call on Tobias. "If he gives you any trouble, don't argue," I told him. My intention, if he didn't pay, was to turn it over to a magistrate.

My man reported the very next day. "There's no such number on the street."

"Are you sure?" I asked, knowing the answer.

"Dead certain," he replied with a grin. Evidently Tobias would open an account with a modest amount, secure the checks, and then close the account before any statements were sent. I'm certain he had some convincing stories to tell the banks. It is almost certain he had a number of bank accounts, and I had a lot of company. He was, however, a very pleasant and charming person to be conned by.

Another client whose company I enjoyed was the co-owner of the Valley Forge Music Fair, a very large theater-in-the-round. He was responsible for quite a few referrals over the years. Many well-known stars and entertainers appeared there, and I had the pleasure of meeting many of them, because they often traveled with their pets in their entourages. Frank Sinatra and Bob Hope were among them.

Joan Blondell, a famous actress way back when I was more impressionable and naive regarding collections, was a referral who took me pretty well. She was performing at the Music Fair for two weeks in a popular play, with two shows nightly. She had a small, fuzzy dog whose breed and name escape me. The dog, brought in by a snooty show biz–type man, was admitted to my hospital with a note from her. Her note, as I recall, described a digestive upset. Now, a dog with diarrhea in a hotel suite is pretty hard to contend with. Giving two performances a night and being entertained by the admiring local gentry leaves the owner little time (or desire) to handle it. Her request was to hospitalize the dog until it was well and to call her or her assistant when the stool was firm.

The dog wasn't seriously ill and a couple of days' treatment effected a cure. Mrs. Walsh called and advised Miss Blondell that the pet could be picked up anytime during office hours. She also mentioned that payment was expected upon discharge and named the amount due. Miss Blondell said she wanted her pet to stay on boarding at the hospital, as we had advised her three pills should be administered daily and she didn't want any responsibility, what with her busy schedule. She also demanded that the dog be walked outside on a leash three times daily, instead of just having a run in our fenced, individual dog yards. There would, of course, be an additional charge for that. She grandly indicated that that was no problem. Of course it wasn't. She had no intention of paying the bill, so the amount was immaterial. I didn't understand at that time that some of those show-biz "glamorous" people feel that anyone who renders them a service should feel privileged to serve them—at no charge. Miss Blondell had accumulated a sizable bill with all her special requests.

When her minion appeared to pick up the dog, Mrs. Walsh presented him with a bill. He, in effect, threw up his hands. "Miss Blondell has already left for her home in Hollywood. She never travels with money. All her bills are paid by her secretary in Hollywood. Simply bill her there." He indicated that he couldn't pay the bill because he was merely an agent, but assured Mrs. Walsh that Miss Blondell's secretary would attend to it.

"But," I protested to Mrs. Walsh, "you warned them the bill must be paid at discharge." I began to understand the magnitude of the problem when Mrs. Walsh said to me in a reverent, hushed tone, "But what could I do? After all, it was Miss Joan Blondell's dog." Apparently her luster was so great that even Mrs. Walsh was affected.

After a few months, I told Mrs. Walsh not to bother sending any more bills. "We're just sending good money after bad."

Mrs. Walsh continued to defend her, though. "The poor dear, she's probably just working too hard, but I'm sure she'll get around to paying someday." Someday, I thought, was beginning to look like forever.

When I mentioned the incident later to my client Shelley Gross, who had referred her, he told me how lucky I was. "You should have seen the hotel bill she stuck the Valley Forge Arms with. In the thousands." Yes, indeed, I guess I had been lucky.

Another case stands out in my memory. This one involved a local attorney whose forte was criminal defense. I recalled reading his name in the papers often, most recently in connection with a particularly unsavory murder case.

My contact with him resulted from an accident. The Lower Merion Township Animal Control Unit brought in the poor mongrel (I prefer the description "all-American") in a really sorry state. He had a fractured femur of the right hind leg, pelvic fractures, a dislocated hip of the left hind leg. The case was obviously going to involve some serious surgery and a long period of hospitalization.

The dog's collar had an ID tag with the name "Lucky" (a poor choice based on that day's accident) and a phone number. I called and spoke with Mrs. Robert Bannion and outlined the situation, explaining the complications and the long hospitalization required if everything were to mend smoothly.

Our policy always was to do everything to get an animal stable as quickly as possible, and if safe, to administer pain suppressors. I did this in all cases, whether the owner was known or not, without authorization or any promise of payment. It was the only merciful way to care for animals. So when I called, Mrs. Bannion's all-American was fairly stable. I explained the case would involve considerable expense.

"By all means, do everything necessary for our Lucky. May my son and I visit after the surgery?" Mrs. Bannion asked.

I usually discouraged that. "It's better not to," I explained.

"We want to keep Lucky as immobile as possible, and the

owner's presence always stimulates a pet to motion, tail wag-
ging, and a struggle to get to their feet to approach and get a
loving pat."

"May I bring in his blanket so he'll feel more at home?"
she asked. I could almost feel the tears being held back.

"Of course," I agreed, thinking how caring she was.

We gave Mrs. Bannion periodic verbal reports on the good
progress our patient was making. The dog was easy to like and
had become a favorite of the staff. We had a long time to get
to know him, because it was a full seven weeks until we could
happily announce Lucky could go home, provided he was
kept on a leash and his activities were strictly limited for another week or two.

Mrs. Bannion and her eight-year-old son arrived for a joyful reunion. All were ecstatic. Mrs. Walsh had presented a
fully detailed bill and been advised that Mrs. Bannion's husband handled all the bills and she would give it to him.

The Main Line area where I practiced was the richest area
of Pennsylvania in per capita income. A large number of my
clients were "charge" accounts. They were accustomed to
saying "Bill me." Many of them were slow to pay, but we did
eventually get the money. I always charged the chronic slow
payers a little more. Today it is customary to add late charges
to bills, and payment at time of service is the norm. Today's
vets are more businesslike.

After sending Mr. Bannion a bill monthly for three months
as was our custom, Mrs. Walsh advised him that we must receive payment within thirty days or we would be forced to take
the matter to small claims court. This usually resulted in payment, but not with Mr. Bannion. I ended up having to go to
Magistrate's Court on this one. The amount was just too large
to let go. I was on time, but Attorney Bannion arrived twenty
minutes late, with no apology for his tardiness, and with a
blue-bound brief and a mute assistant. Although he was usually a defense lawyer, he was all prosecutor at our hearing.

He demanded that I be sworn in and that he be permitted

to cross-examine me. "Did you ever see me before, or have you ever talked to me before?"

"No," I answered.

"Then, Your Honor, how could I have any contract with this man? He is claiming I breached a contract. Not so. None existed."

It was too costly for me to retain a lawyer for claims court, so I addressed the court directly. "Your Honor [a courtesy title, as he was not a judge], it was an implied contract. The fact that he didn't remove the dog and permitted me to continue treatment for almost two months was to me an implied contract." The magistrate agreed with me.

The barrister consulted his blue-bound brief and was handed a paper by his assistant. "Your Honor, this man is a robber. Here on his itemized bill are charges for six X-rays at fifteen dollars apiece. All his other charges are equally outrageous.

"What, Dr. Scanlon," he continued, now addressing me, "does an X-ray film cost you?"

"About a dollar," I replied.

"Actually, Your Honor, it's more like eighty-five cents," said Bannion, looking at his enormous brief. I was amazed at the trouble he had gone to (or perhaps the ever-mute assistant had done it).

The magistrate nodded at me, indicating it was my turn to talk. I was trying not to let my disgust with Bannion show, but I'm afraid a little sarcasm may have leaked out. "The film cost is minor," I said to the court. "As I'm sure Your Honor realizes, but Mr. Bannion obviously doesn't, in a professional office, the knowledge is the expensive part. In order to get a useful X-ray, the dog must be positioned perfectly, the film must be perfectly developed, and someone with the appropriate education must read it." Looking at his assistant, I continued, "I have help who must be paid, taxes, and overhead. X-rays cannot be taken for the cost of the film, any more than a legal brief can be prepared for the cost of the paper. Your Honor will find that my fees are very much in line with my

colleagues' and not at all outrageous." I had included as part
of my preparation a list of comparable fees from other veterinary hospitals.

The magistrate took a very serious and comprehensive
look at my bill and comparison sheets. He nodded and said,
"These fees seem reasonable enough."

At this point, Bannion, who hadn't done that well so far,
played what he must have seen as his trump card. "Are you
aware, Your Honor, that the owner of this dog is my son, who
is a minor? You cannot under the law sue a minor. I request
this case be dismissed."

The magistrate looked at him with distaste and then turned
to me. Whenever I went to the magistrate, which was rarely, I
took along a file containing all records and related papers.
Fortunately, Mrs. Walsh had saved a note of thanks written
shortly after Lucky was discharged to his home. I removed the
note from the file and handed it to the magistrate, comment-
ing that Mrs. Bannion had used the words "my dog" in her
kind note to me. I said a silent "thank you" to Mrs. Bannion
for her note and to Mrs. Walsh for her habit of saving all
scraps of paper.

The magistrate read it, banged his gavel, and with a grin at
the attorney announced, "Judgment is awarded for the full bill
plus court costs to Dr. Scanlon. A husband is responsible for
his wife's bills. That is the law."

The attorney was livid. "Your Honor, may I speak privately
with Dr. Scanlon?"

"Permission granted," replied the pleased and still-
grinning magistrate. He didn't seem to like Bannion much
more than I did.

We went to the back of the courtroom, and he thrust his
face into mine. He had not used his toothbrush or morning
mouthwash. "See here, Scanlon. This isn't over. I plan to appeal to the next higher court. That will cost you money and
you'll have to pay a lawyer. I'm gonna be generous and give
you the chance to settle for half your bill right now."

He was becoming detestable to me. Here was a man prostituting his profession for only one purpose: to cheat me out of my fair and hard-earned fees. I believed what he said. He was just nasty enough to put me through an appeal and legal expenses. But no way was I going to let this legal bully get his way.

I lied. I advised him that an appeal was fine with me and that I had a brother-in-law who was an attorney and would represent me at no cost. "What's his name?" he demanded. "Well, Mr. Bannion, you'll meet him in court soon enough and you will certainly recognize him then." I turned my back on him and departed. The bluff and lie worked. I received a check for the full amount within the week.

There was a far more famous attorney who was also convinced that bills were to be sent to the wastepaper basket. Lemuel B. Schofield was a nationally known attorney who, through some official appointment, had "freedom of the port." This meant he could enter and leave the country without the formality of customs inspection.

He was married, but lived apart from his wife. "She's a fine person, a strict Roman Catholic who doesn't believe in divorce," my reliable gossip Mrs. Walsh imparted. "That Countess he consorts with cannot hold a candle to Mr. Schofield's lovely wife."

It was the Countess, an overwhelmingly handsome and overbearing woman, who was actually my client. She was frequently accompanied on her visits to my office by Lemuel B. Mrs. Walsh was told to send all bills to his Center City office. The Countess was difficult to deal with and told me with authority that her two dachshunds, Ping and Pong, should be examined monthly. I suggested that they were young and in excellent health and that perhaps there was no need for such frequent exams.

"I want a standing appointment the first Wednesday morning of every month at 11:30 A.M. That will give me time to make a noon luncheon at the General Wayne Inn with my friends," she explained.

It was quite plain who was the dominant partner in this relationship. On one visit, Lemuel slipped a small piece of candy from his vest pocket (decorated, by the way, with a Phi Beta Kappa key) to his mouth. It didn't escape the Countess, who glared at his ample stomach and accused him of being "a pig and fat" and ordered him to stop snacking. Lemuel took a paper towel from my sink, spat out the candy, and deposited it in the trash can without protest. He didn't seem embarrassed by his consort's domineering and demanding tone.

The Countess had a Center City art gallery and was known as an interior decorator to the wealthy. Mrs. Walsh, ever suspicious, suggested that Lemuel, having freedom of the port, had smuggled in artworks for the Countess. Perhaps they were partners in smuggling, she went on. "She must have something on him, because no man would put up with that bossy a woman." I tended to agree.

I should note here that my ever-eager trivia collector had positioned and repositioned her desk on more than one occasion to ensure that all voices, loud or soft, would carry clearly to her command position. We had a pass-through in the wall that was an additional aid. Mrs. Walsh had the ability to talk to a waiting client, do paperwork, and hear (analyze and file) what was going on in my examining room, all at the same time. Today's computer generation thinks it invented "multi-tasking," but Mrs. Walsh set the standard four decades ago.

The Countess was ever faithful and punctual with her pets' appointment, on the first Wednesday of every month. I considered it a waste of time but examined each little dog thoroughly under her watchful eye. They were delightful animals, with glowing red coats and exuberant dispositions. I enjoyed their visits, trying to avoid their avid kisses as I checked their eyes, ears, oral cavities, and skin. I listened to their hearts and lungs, took their temperatures, cut their nails, and cleaned out their ears.

After about seven monthly check-ups, vaccinations, and some lab work, the bills were mounting. It was becoming apparent that the eminent Lemuel B. Schofield, Esquire, was another potential deadbeat. Calls to his office were not fruitful. His secretary was skilled at evasion. When she asked when we could expect payment, Mrs. Walsh was advised what a busy court schedule the boss had.

In this case, though, I had some leverage. I contacted the high and mighty one and told her we would have to cancel her next month's scheduled appointment. "You positively cannot do that to my Ping and Pong. They love you. I've had them to other vets and you are the only one who understands them."

This was news to me. "Countess," I explained, "I will refer you and their records to a competent veterinarian, but I cannot continue to treat them without being paid. It seems Mr. Schofield ignores my bills and we have not received even a single payment."

"What?!" she shrieked. "That son of a bitch. Give me the amount due and you will be paid before the day is out. Tomorrow morning at the latest."

I buzzed the intercom for Mrs. Walsh. My, how she was going to enjoy talking to the irate royalty. "Mrs. Walsh does the bookkeeping and I will turn you over to her."

The Countess's voice was still strident. "Thank you. I will see you with my dear Ping and Pong as usual."

As promised, someone from Lemuel's office appeared before the day was over, bearing an envelope with the exact amount in cash. The bearer requested a receipt and was on his way. Such was the power of the Countess over her consort.

The Countess called me early on a Sunday morning in late May. It was a beautiful day, and I had planned to do some flower planting and yard clean-up. The Countess had bullied Mrs. Walsh into giving her my home number, which was now unlisted.

"There is always a doctor available, Countess. We offer twenty-four-hour emergency service," Mrs. Walsh had countered the request.

"But my dear Mrs. Walsh, I permit only Dr. Scanlon to care

for them, and he might not be on duty if I ever had an emergency."

She was calling from Lemuel's Chester County farm. It seemed his barn dog had become entangled in some barbed wire and while the injury was not terribly serious, the Squire (as she called him) felt it should be attended to as soon as possible. As an additional incentive, I was to join them for brunch before or after my treatment. Actually, I was curious to see the famous country estate and Lemuel's well-known herd of Brown Swiss cattle. It would be about a half-hour's drive each way, and I should be home in time to do the gardening I had planned.

"What about the vet who usually cares for his dog?" I asked, ever mindful of professional courtesy.

"He's out of town, unavailable. Please come. I'm serving eggs Benedict and whiskey sours or Bloody Marys." This was a different Countess, actually asking instead of commanding. Of course, I agreed.

The estate lived up to its billing. The barns and outbuildings were designed and built after the Swiss farm motif. The manor house was more like the Southern Plantation style, but all was harmonious. The wide verandas and white pillars shouted "wealthy gentleman farmer" and "tax deductible." There was no way the magnificent Brown Swiss cattle could pay for the beautifully landscaped, fenced, lush pastures or the elegant house.

The patient, as I had suspected, required very little, and only elementary, wound attention. I cleaned a little, cauterized, put in a few sutures, and gave a penicillin injection. A tetanus shot wasn't needed. Tetanus is very rarely a problem in canines.

The Countess was pouring coffee from an obviously precious urn. "Cream? Sugar?" She was a charming hostess as I indulged in a perfect whiskey sour and the promised eggs Benedict, all served by an elderly maid. The Countess, dressed in a slightly revealing gown, was directing a considerable amount of the table talk my way. Was she just being the good hostess, trying to make me comfortable, or did I detect the undertones of a flirting female—the occasional batting eyelashes, the smiles, the direct looks? Certainly this was a side of her I never suspected.

The Squire, attired in an expensive, lightweight robe, was occupied with scanning the *New York Times* Sunday edition. There were several other papers on the large table. He either didn't care or didn't pay attention to her while she directed what seemed to be more than a hostess's attention to me. She was at least ten years his junior and I was roughly ten years her junior. I was uncomfortable, and relieved when she announced she had several phone calls to make and intended to dress for the day.

Squire Schofield and I were left alone at the table sipping a final cup of coffee. "Want to look at the papers?" he asked as he pushed the *Philadelphia Inquirer* toward me and continued to read his own. To my surprise, the big headlines of the lead story shouted "Schofield to Defend Chief Magistrate O'Malley."

I was aware, as were all *Inquirer* readers, that Chief Magistrate O'Malley was under indictment for tax evasion and bribery and a lot more. I was also aware from the papers that Lemuel had defended a number of well-known evaders with good results over the years. He was a considered a specialist in that field.

"Counselor," I said. "I see you are on page one and will be defending O'Malley."

He looked at me over his Franklin glasses and with a semi-scowl said, "Yes. I seem to get stuck with these cases. Actually, I dislike them. If it weren't for the fees and publicity, I would turn them down. Of course, we attorneys owe them representation. A man's duty to his country is to pay his taxes."

This pious statement was amazing in view of what happened about two years later. The headlines then read "Prominent Lawyer Lemuel B. Schofield Dead of Massive Heart Attack." In smaller but very prominent type, the story continued: "An informant reveals his failure to file federal or state income taxes for many years." The informant's name was not disclosed.

It was clear that in death Lemuel B. had provided for his Countess. An informant's fee, it was explained to me, came out of the estate, taking precedence over all other creditors. Thus, his wife, his children, and all other debtors with their claims were behind the Countess. Lemuel had obviously advised her to "drop a dime" on him, because otherwise, she had no claims to his estate.

Of course, in these times of computers it would be impossible for a man of his wealth and prominence to get away with this clever maneuver. But back then, if the government had never received a filed tax form, you didn't exist. No wonder he was in demand as a tax evader's attorney. He was one of the best. The Countess must have received a huge informant's fee. With years and years of no payment plus interest, it is conceivable that she received a very large chunk of his holdings.

An invitation from the Countess for an intimate dinner at her luxurious hotel suite was not entirely unexpected shortly after the Sunday breakfast. I declined, claiming a previous engagement. She was a very worldly woman, and no other invitation was forthcoming. We continued to give Ping and Pong their monthly exams after the Squire's death and my fees were always paid promptly. I'm sure the source of the funds was the estate of Lemuel B. Schofield, Esquire.

At the time of my retirement, my practice had more than $400,000 in uncollected fees, most of them beyond hope, and many of them from people far wealthier than I. My overall feeling is that people with average incomes were easier to deal with. They seemed to take their debts more seriously. The state of the receivables was a testament to my poor business methods and the public's cleverness.

eleven

Cops and Robbers

The intercom buzzed: "A Kathleen Sullivan on line one," announced a chipper Mrs. Walsh.

I sat down. "Hello, Kathy, how are you?"

"Just fine," the madam of the finest "house" in Philadelphia replied. "How's your practice going?"

I had recently made the big move, left my secure job at the SPCA and hung out my shingle. Kathy and I were always frank, so I told her honestly, "It's not easy, but I'll make it. I had a little left over this month, but we're still eating hamburger and scratching."

"Well, I think maybe I can help you out a little. One of our johns is in charge of the Fairmount Park police dogs. He commented on how great my dogs look, and I talked to him about you and how you saved them after that knife attack. I told him no one could do better by his dogs than you." I brightened up. The Philadelphia police, of which the Fairmount Park Police were part, had a large number of trained dogs. They were used for attack and riot control as well as for patrol. Their care would involve annual exams, vaccinations, and lab work for heartworm and intestinal parasites. With such a large kennel, there would be other veterinary needs as well.

Knowing the corruption that the Philadelphia police were known for, I asked, "What's the payoff?"

Kathy laughed. "I think you're in luck. The captain really loves his dogs and dislikes their present vet. Says he's sloppy and incompetent. He's also crazy over my girls, so a little free trade will probably take care of it. Of course, you'd be expected to give him a case of booze and a Christmas present. No big deal."

I was elated at the prospect of such a potential windfall. "That would really be a plum for me. We'll be able to add an occasional steak to our hamburger diet, and get something new for the baby's nursery. Kathy, I can't thank you enough. I owe you one."

"You owe me nothing. That's what friends are for. Stop by for a chat and a cup of tea when you're in the neighborhood."

Sure enough, Captain Sean O'Brien called me within the week. I set up an appointment to be interviewed at the Fairmount Park Dog Kennels and Stables.

Captain O'Brien was an example of why stereotypes get started. He was the archetypal Irish cop: large, florid, with the peat bogs written on his face, he had short, cropped gray hair and a square jaw. He was pugnacious and had a drinker's ruddy complexion. He looked me over slowly. "Scanlon. Scanlon. You're Irish?"

I returned his gaze. "Yes, and proud of it."

"You're a friend of Kathy's?"

"Yes. I take care of her dogs."

"When can you start?"

"Anytime you say."

Probably the shortest job interview in history—certainly the shortest in my experience. I was now the official vet to the police dogs. Kathy had been right. I was relieved. There had been no allusions to a payoff—very unusual. He did order me on my way out, "They are all due for their annual exam. Meet me here at two tomorrow for lunch."

He was equally to the point the following day. "You are not to handle any of these dogs without a muzzle. Most are attack-trained, and I don't want to be sued by a fellow Irishman." That suited me. They were mostly German shepherds with large fangs. There were some equally well-armed Dobermans. We discussed my ideas of what an annual exam should consist of, and he agreed with my proposals. "You can only examine three every afternoon. I need them on the street," he ordered.

"Okay, I'll schedule them to suit you and their handler." In fact, some of the dogs spent little time at the kennel and actually lived with childless officers. I was aware my predecessor had usually vetted them at the police kennel. "The only thing I ask," I continued, "is that the handlers bring them to my hospital at the scheduled time."

"What the hell do you mean? The other guy examined them here. That's the way we do it." He glared at me. "My officers would lose travel time your way."

I glared back, knowing I needed to establish some control at the start. "Captain, you know I can do a better job at my place. I just explained how thorough the exam needs to be to ensure your animals stay in peak condition. Besides, my fees are less at my hospital."

Sean had a short temper and was accustomed to giving orders, not taking them. "You'll do them here, same as the other guy," he commanded.

I needed the fees badly, but I was Irish too. "Maybe you want the other guy back?"

He was purple-faced. *God,* I thought, *I'm blowing it. The steak is turning back into hamburger.*

He turned his back to me and spat. After a silent moment he turned. "Okay, Scanlon, you're the doc. We'll do it your way." Thank God I had won the first battle. I didn't win every future battle, but when the dogs' welfare was involved, Sean would usually surrender, although not always gracefully.

Every month, I mentally thanked Kathy. My fees were paid promptly, and they were considerable. Without them, there would have been many dull, fruitless hours at my new, mostly empty hospital. I got along well with the handlers, which was another plus. Their names escape me, but, predictably, many were Irish. They often recommended me to their pet-owning friends, and my practice was growing.

Another battle I had with Sean was dubbed by my wife the Tooth Battle. Many of the dogs had been in service five or more years, and their teeth were coated with tartar. The previous vet had given little, if any, dental care, and the dogs' gums were inflamed. I pointed their condition out to Sean and the battle was on. "They need a thorough cleaning and scaling to remove the build-up. I'll put them under a light general anesthetic," I advised.

"That's horse shit, Scanlon. Everyone knows dogs don't get cavities."

I shot back at him, "True, but they do get periodontal disease, and they do get abscessed teeth from tartar. It can separate the tooth from its blood supply."

By this time I was staring at Sean's forehead veins, which were standing out clearly in his anger. "Maybe you're just trying to increase your outrageous fees. The other guy never did any such crap."

The reference to the "other guy" was the last straw. He could really fire me up. "Look, O'Brien, you're a police captain, not a veterinarian. You may think you have the last say, but you have a boss too." Angry, I really sank to a new low. "I'm sure Kathy can tell me his name."

His short temper was flaring. I braced myself; he looked like he was about to throw a punch. "You son of a bitch," he yelled. "You'd go over my head?"

"Yes, I would, for the sake of the dogs. They can end up in pain and needing teeth pulled. It isn't right."

Fortunately, a nearby sergeant intervened. "Look, guys, we're supposed to be grown-ups. Don't be stupid, don't get out of line." We looked at each other and realized the sarge was right. Sean walked away. After a cooling-off period, both of us apologized.

"Doc, I'm sorry. I have a teenage son driving me crazy. You don't suggest unnecessary work. I know that. Go ahead," he smiled. "Play dentist."

I offered my hand. "Pardon my unprofessional conduct," I said. If he could be big, so could I. "You always see your dogs get the best, whatever they need." We both felt awkward, sheepish, and glad the battle was over.

I had occasion to make a house call at Kathy's soon after I cleaned the police dogs' teeth, and during our tea, I described the incident to her. "He has one bad temper, and he's dangerous when he's been drinking," she commented. "I never told you, but he was the guy who introduced us."

I looked puzzled. "You mean he was the john who cut up your dogs?"

"He's the one. That was the only time he got out of line in all the years he's been coming to me. Otherwise, I'd never have allowed him back. He has a very bad marriage, a son into drugs." She sipped her tea. "I guess we're all entitled to snap, once anyway."

"Vetting" the police dogs was sometimes challenging, as they were "one-man" dogs. They had no respect for anyone but their handlers, and they refused to respond to anyone else's commands. In later years, with the advent of a wide choice of excellent tranquilizers, they would have been easier to handle. The rare occasions when I had to hospitalize a dog for a long period were especially worrisome. I had to be careful for myself and my kennel help, as the dogs were truly dangerous.

Jumbo, an attack dog, once had a fight with a "streetwise" stray dog. I wouldn't want to meet that stray, as he had left the mighty Jumbo with a fracture of the left foreleg and numerous infected bite wounds. There was no problem with reducing and casting the fracture or cleaning and suturing the wounds. These procedures were done under a general anesthetic. The challenge was how to administer the daily antibiotic injections and drain and tend the infected wounds when he was awake.

I asked the captain to arrange to keep him at the police kennel and have him brought to my hospital daily. Jumbo was 110 pounds, a mean, touchy German shepherd. No way did I want to hospitalize him.

Sean was in another feisty mood. "Look, Doc, I can't keep him here. His handler is going on vacation. We're short-handed. I can't spare anyone." I could feel his resentment. "He's your problem. That's what you get paid for."

The captain had a point; it was my problem. "Okay, Sean, I'll handle it." With no other option, I'd best be agreeable.

Sean's feeling of victory was almost visible. "I'm sure you'll get along fine, Doc. At heart, Jumbo is a pussycat." He chuckled and repeated, "A real pussycat." Why wasn't I reassured?

Since I couldn't expose my kennel people to his jaws, I took over Jumbo's daily care. And he introduced me to a cheap, surefire, no-side-effects tranquilizer.

Water was never offered to patients until the day after surgery, due to nausea. The morning after Jumbo's surgery, I approached his pen with a dish of fresh water and food. When I opened the door a crack, he came at me, fangs exposed, undeterred by the cast on his broken leg. He meant business. I slammed the door shut. The same performance was repeated at noon, but he seemed less aggressive. I knew he was becoming slightly dehydrated. When I approached again with water at about 4 P.M., he showed only mild interest in attacking me, but I, not the water, was still his primary focus.

After evening hours, about 8:30, I again approached and placed the water next to his pen. He now wagged his tail and sniffed. I had found the tranquilizer. It was cheap and didn't have to be injected. I opened the pen door and gave him the water. He gave me a weak growl, but thirstily and quickly lapped up the small amount I offered. I retrieved the bowl, filled it up, and returned it to his pen. No growl, just a slight tail wag. We now understood each other. He was no problem for the rest of his stay. The water-giver, I discovered, could control even the most dangerous attack dogs.

The police dogs were my patients for a number of years. Although they were a potential danger to me, capable of inflicting severe bites, they never bit me. In fact, in over forty years of pet treatment, I was bitten only a few times. Dangerous or vicious dogs are the safest to handle because the vet knows their potential for harm.

I have no figures or statistics, but would guess that zoo vets and circus vets have the best safety record of all. They just assume all their patients are potentially dangerous. I was bitten only by "sweet dogs," supposed non-biters. I had assumed that the few whose teeth penetrated my flesh were sweethearts. "Not a mean bone," according to their loving owners.

The only time I suffered a serious bite was due to my trusting an owner and to my own carelessness. I can still find the scars on my ears. The biter was a Great Dane bitch. She had delivered, in a normal fashion, ten pups. Her uterus, exhausted, had lost its tone and its contractile powers. After examining her, I knew she still had another pup. I believed that with the injection of a uterine-contracting stimulant and some forceps help on my part, we could avoid a cesarean section.

She was nasty by temperament, and with pain, I knew she would bite. I was reluctant to muzzle her, as doing so would shut off her panting and impair her sweating process. A dog has no sweat glands, and panting acts as the body's coolant.

I found an answer. "Mr. Costello," I directed her owner, "wrap your arm around her neck like a wrestler. That way she can't turn and bite me." The bitch was standing and I was kneeling, face level with the vaginal orifice. My sterile forceps in my gloved hand were ready to deliver the dead pup.

She had renewed mild, definite contractions, and it would be all over in a moment. I placed the forceps around the dead pup's head and gently began to withdraw it. At this point, my "assistant" let go of his headlock to check on my progress. The next thing I knew, half my face and head were between the dog's jaws. I was literally looking at her tonsils. She ripped one ear badly as I extricated myself. The owner reapplied his headlock, sparing me further bites, but one had been enough. Later I had to visit Bryn Mawr Hospital's emergency room for stitches to repair my mangled ear. I sent Mr. Costello his bill, along with the cleaning bill for my new suit. I had been careless not to keep an eye on Mr. Costello, and he had failed me. But, hey, only one bite requiring stitches in forty years! A very small price to pay. I'm sorry to say I know of two equine vets who were seriously injured by horses. One paid the ultimate price—death from a fractured skull.

Years later I gave up the police dog work. Sean was promoted to a soft job with no authority over the canine corps. (His drug-addicted son was serving ten years for dealing.) The new man in charge found a vet willing to pay the extortion money to get the job. When I complained to Sean, he just laughed. "Ed, the new guy will just pad his bills. So could you if you wanted to continue. From what Kathy tells me, you don't need the work. You have two vets working for you, right? You're not hungry like the old days. That's good."

I knew that in his way Sean liked and respected me. His laugh roared. "Think of all the money I lost to you over the years. All you saved. Hey, stop by and say hello. I'll buy you a drink. I'm gonna miss you." I respected his unadmitted love of and dedication to the welfare of his dogs. Age and an easier job would surely mellow his temper. I told him I'd take him up on his invitation, and I did. Time did indeed mellow him, and our occasional drinks together were pleasant.

About that time politics in Philadelphia changed when the new reform mayor, Richardson Dilworth, was elected. While I had known him as a good client, he turned out to be bad news for the police department, and worse for Kathy. He was elected by citizens sick of the rampant corruption and vice. He used a broad broom and many changes for the better occurred.

Kathy called to say good-bye. "They shut me down. That damn fool mayor knows he can't get rid of the houses. He just picked on the biggest and best." I was curious what her plans were. "I'm moving back to Baltimore. I still have connections there, and the mayor knows how to run a decent city." I wished her luck and thanked her for the referrals, the police work, and the friendship. "If you're ever in Baltimore, stop by. I'm taking the old teapot."

I never got to Baltimore. I don't approve of prostitution, but I approved of Kathy.

twelve

Wise Guys

There was a healthy, balanced relationship between the mob figures, the police, and the citizens when I was growing up in West Philadelphia, back before the age of hard drugs. The local mobster was a nice guy. You could bet a dime or a quarter on the day's number, similar to today's legalized lotteries. You could make a bet on the horse race. He cheerfully paid the winner and commiserated with the ones who just missed. He was a good family man. His kids went to school with us. If you couldn't borrow money and were desperate, you could find the local shylock. If you couldn't pay on time, he would carry you, on exorbitant interest rates, "six for five, weekly" (not a whole lot higher than the rates on today's credit cards).

They were just part of the neighborhood; they were accepted. So were the corrupt police. Our next-door neighbor and landlord, Officer Kelly, was well liked. We were proud of him. He was the "bag man" for the precinct, entrusted by the local mob to collect and turn in the bags of protection money the merchants paid. No one remarked on or wondered how he could own two other houses on the block on a patrolman's salary. It was just a fact of life. A neighbor, a widow with two teenage sons headed for trouble, maybe even jail, called Officer Kelly, not the priest or the minister. Two-parent families with similar troubles consulted Kelly. He knew how to solve their problems.

Despite the fact that the mobsters fit in and were accepted, everyone knew they had a dark, sinister side.

Silvio Lanzetti was in some ways similar to an old Roman coin. His leonine head, aquiline nose, and strong, jutting jaws were Caesar-like. Philadelphians valued him as a restaurateur par excellence, a superior host, and a hugely successful businessman. He was widely respected in the Italian community. His restaurant, the Neapolitan, featured superb Italian cuisine. It was always crowded: The finest food, the professional fast service, and the modest prices guaranteed its popularity.

The combination of Lanzetti's low prices and the choice of his companions, known mob figures, led Philadelphia detectives to look at the other side of the coin. They viewed him at best as mob-affiliated and at worst as a laundry for dirty money. In those days, the terms *Mafia* and *La Cosa Nostra* were seldom used. The gangsters were referred to as mobsters or as members of the mob.

Silvio had never been indicted or even arrested. His cousin Pius Lanzetti was gunned down on a street corner, and Pius's brother was also mob-murdered. Silvio was questioned at length about these crimes, and he was most cooperative, but nothing ever came of it.

I had no direct contact with him. His wife, Dolores, always made the appointments with me for the care of their two Siamese cats, India and China. At that time, I was doing everything possible to cut out house calls. My practice had grown to the point where they weren't good business. "We can do a better job at the hospital" was the truth, and I was quite proud of my now up-to-date facility, the Narberth Animal

Hospital. I still made a few house calls for insistent longtime clients or in emergencies.

The Lanzetti cats were in the old clients category. Their home in the "Little Italy" section of South Philadelphia was modest outside, but inside it was opulent. Rare Persian rugs, authentic antique furniture, silver, crystal chandeliers—all spelled wealth.

My mission on house calls was to tend to the patient. The owners and their trappings were just incidental and were ignored where possible. Sometimes, though, it was impossible to overlook the surroundings. The Lanzetti home was overwhelming.

Mrs. Walsh indicated the blinking telephone lines. "Surprise," she said. "It's Philadelphia's Gourmet King."

"Who?"

"Silvio Lanzetti himself."

Was Dolores ill? Was there an emergency? I had never, over the many years of treating the little Siamese terrors, spoken with or met the man.

"Doc, how are you? Silvio Lanzetti here."

"Just fine. Thank you." Why the small talk?

"We have the greatest poached salmon lunch in town. I'd like you to be my guest tomorrow at the Neapolitan. I'd like to talk to you."

"Well, I'm sort of busy. In fact, I rarely go out to lunch. The work just backs up too much. I appreciate the offer, but could we talk now?"

A pause. "Well, Doc, it will also be like a consultation. You'll be paid."

I paused to think. His request was odd and out of the blue. "I really am tied up and it will get hopeless if I leave the office. I will be glad to fit you in here anytime that's convenient for you."

And then the cat popped out of the bag. "Doc, I'd also consider it a returned favor. I did one for you on that police dog contract. I recommended you to that crazy Mick, O'Brien."

The pieces dropped into place. At that time, the police dogs had been my patients for several years. I had questioned Kathy's earlier assertion that a "little free trade" was all Sean O'Brien needed in the way of a kickback. I was hungry then, more naive, and ready to accept her explanation. Now the truth came together. It was Lanzetti who had cemented the contract, probably at Kathy's behest. Her contribution was just a "kicker." That fit the facts and made sense.

According to mob tradition, I didn't "owe him one." Kathy had solicited his help, not me. I pointed it out. "I never knew of your involvement, Mr. Lanzetti." But it was a fine line, neither black nor white.

He countered, his tone hardening, "Maybe so. Look, we can make it a dinner meeting if that suits you better." He was determined that we meet privately, and his consultation request was obviously fishy. I knew it was stupid, even dangerous, to have any association with the mob, but perhaps my growing up in West Philadelphia with a mob figure on every corner made me careless. After all, he was a longtime, prompt-paying client, asking for a consultation. I shouldn't prejudge him.

"Let's make it lunch. I'll make some changes in my schedule," I answered.

The jovial host voice returned. "Doc, that's great. You'll love the salmon."

It was indeed delicious, sprinkled with fresh herbs. So was my glass of imported Chianti wine. He was a most gracious host—an entertaining storyteller with a flair for the unexpected punchline. Finally, he got around to business. "Doc, you handled all the Philadelphia police dogs for a couple years." He sipped his wine and moved his face closer. "You understand this consultation is strictly confidential, just between us." It was not a question. I nodded.

"How many sniffers do they have?"

I questioned him, "You mean the dogs the drug squad uses for detecting—" I paused, searching for a euphemism—"contraband stuff?"

"Yes," he said with emphasis, "contraband stuff."

"Mr. Lanzetti, I don't know, but I would guess only two or three. They are so highly trained, specialized."

It was now "Call me Silvio" time. "That's it, Doc? Just a couple?"

"Silvio, that's just a guess. Most of them are just attack- and riot control–trained. Why do you ask?"

He moved even closer. "Now, just suppose you wanted to make them useless for sniffing. How could you do that? How would you take away their sense of smell?" I drew back. "How about a drug? You must know of something." I didn't answer, just looked back at him. "Doc, you're the top vet in town. You worked with these dogs. Surely you know how to disarm them."

"Silvio, I don't know of any drug. There are local anes- thetics, some aerosol sprays that might temporarily numb their sense of smell." My apprehension was growing.

The purpose of his "consultation" was now clear. The use of illicit drugs then was minuscule by today's standards. How- ever, it was known that the mob was becoming increasingly interested and active in the dirty business.

"Isn't there something that you could put in their food?" Clearly he had been thinking about this.

"Absolutely not. There is nothing short of surgery that will destroy their sense of smell." I wanted to end this now very uncomfortable conversation.

Silvio was not giving up. "Doc, there has got to be some- thing."

"Look, Mr. Lanzetti, I have no expertise in destroying a dog's ability to scent. Even if there were such a drug, and I emphasize there is not, I'd have no part in using it." It was time for me to draw the line.

One last effort on his part, the carrot. "Doc, anything that would do the job would be near priceless. We were counting on you."

I stood up, now afraid of a possible stick. "I told you I

know of no such thing. Maybe a professor of pharmacology knows of something." As I was saying it, I knew better. "Thanks for the lunch. The consultation is free." I walked out disgusted and feeling a little despoiled.

Returning to the hospital, I directed Mrs. Walsh, "If Dolores Lanzetti calls, tell her flat out I don't make house calls anymore. She's welcome to bring them here or I'll transfer their records to another vet."

She raised her elegant eyebrows and smiled a knowing smile. "Hmm, our luncheon didn't go so well? A little indigestion?" She read me well, no secrets easily kept. But I knew her, and recognized her gossip-gathering mode. I was on to her and she couldn't pump me. We had the perfect working relationship.

Silvio did reappear on two more occasions. The first was not unpleasant. He phoned several weeks after our luncheon. He was brief: "Doc, you were right. Anything that might do the job doesn't exist. There's no such animal. I told my connections you were tops in your field. They just spun their wheels."

His second appearance was anything but pleasant. He was waiting in the parking area in a new silver Cadillac. Obviously, he had timed his visit to coincide with the end of my day's office hours.

"Get in, Doc. I gotta talk to you." Gone was the smooth, at-ease host. The door was open; I couldn't back away.

"I only have a few minutes, Silvio. My wife has dinner waiting."

He smiled. "No problem, I only need a couple minutes." I was uncomfortable, but sat down.

"Doc, you're a lucky guy, you don't have a boss like most people." He pushed in the cigarette lighter, lit up. "Now I have a dear friend, he's also a kind of Boss." I could hear the capital *B* in *Boss,* and I started to get more nervous.

"Please, Silvio, get to the point."

"I told him about you, how you are the best." He sensed

my impatience. "Doc, this is strictly professional. He wants you to look over, fix his favorite dog. She is nursing a litter and just isn't doing well. The pups aren't right either."

"Well," I said, reaching to open the door, "he must have a good vet. I have all the business I can handle."

He quickly placed his hand over the door handle. "You don't understand. You don't turn down someone like him." His hand prevented my exit. "I can't deny him. You may not agree, but I feel you still owe me. I'm asking for a big favor." I looked pointedly at his hand, preventing me from reaching the door handle. "Look, Doc, I promise," and here he crossed himself, "I'll never ask another."

After thinking it over, I agreed. After all, he had probably been responsible for my having a solid source of income while I built my practice. "I'll do it, under two conditions. I'll make one, and only one, visit, and I'm not taking him on as a client. I'll see the patient tomorrow about noon, after Sunday church. And, Silvio, I don't, and never did, owe you one."

He removed his hand, reached for mine. "It's a deal, Doc. I'll spell it out, just as you say."

I was not happy, but it didn't spoil my dinner with my wife and girls.

He picked me up at the hospital on time, and I carried two black bags. One was filled with as wide a variety of drugs as I thought could possibly be needed. Heaven knew what the problem was, as the described symptoms, "not doing well," couldn't have been more vague. I wanted to be prepared for anything, as I was not going to go back.

It turned out his friend and "kind of Boss" lived near New Hope, Pennsylvania, a fairly long drive. Silvio clued me in a little on his friend. "The Don . . . Mr. De Cavalante is as fine a person as you'll ever meet. He's a Harvard Law School graduate, although he doesn't practice." His slip, "The Don," would have impressed me more had I read *The Godfather*, but Mario Puzo had not yet written his bestseller. Nevertheless, I was generally aware of the term and its implication.

He continued, "He loves fox terriers, the smooth-coated kind, and raises an occasional litter. The sick one, the mother, is his favorite."

I was curious. "Well, if he doesn't practice law, what does he do?"

Silvio waved it off. "Oh, investments, like real estate, and several businesses." He lit another initialed cigarette. "He has a piece of the Neapolitan. I know you'll like him."

He was right. The man was very likable. Mr. De Cavalante was the picture of a loving grandfather, even to the point of playing ball on the estate's lawn with several grandchildren when we arrived. He was cordial, polite, and charming, making me feel like an honored guest whose arrival had been anxiously anticipated. He had a round, almost wrinkle-free face, contrasted by full, pure white hair and a closely trimmed, snowy mustache. "So nice of you to come, to attend my little Stella."

"Mr. De Cavalante, despite what Silvio may have told you, I'm not a magician. It might well be that your vet is doing, or has already done, everything possible." We were on the wide verandah. "Before I examine her, let's talk about her symptoms and medical history."

His anxiety about his little Stella was thick in the air, but his courteous nature was such that he wouldn't continue until I was comfortably seated and had been given a beverage.

"Well, she just isn't acting right." It seemed Silvio had been quoting his Boss accurately. I needed more. My prodding questions brought out a fuller symptomatic picture. "She eats erratically, very picky about food, and that's just not like her, Doc. She's a good little eater normally. Sometimes she nurses her pups, other times she shoves them aside. Again, completely different than with her last litter. Sometimes she trembles like she's cold, but she hasn't been running a fever."

"How old is she?" I asked, pen and pad in hand. They were more for Silvio's benefit than for mine. He was standing nearby, almost fawning.

"She's just about eight years old," he replied. I paused and sternly told him this had better be her last litter, that she was too old. He lowered his head. "Yes, that's what the other vet said. It's just that my grandchildren . . ." His voice trailed off.

"When did she deliver, and was there any difficulty?"

"Two weeks ago with no problems."

"Has she had any previous health problems?"

He gave thoughtful consideration to my questions. "No. She has always been hearty."

"What has your other vet done, and has he made any diagnosis?"

"He sort of says it's her age. That's why I wanted another opinion. There's something more wrong. I know my Stella. He's given her vitamins, minerals, and an appetite stimulant. But she's going downhill." He looked discouraged. "I hope you can help her."

It was time to examine the little mother and pups. He led me to a spacious study. The patient and four wriggling pups, their eyes barely opened, were ensconced in a large whelping pen. I stopped to admire them before going to work. Stella was a beautiful specimen of the breed, real show quality. Fox terriers have always been a personal favorite of mine. Our current family dog is one. The pups are irresistible and these were very nice indeed—the spotted black and white variety.

Stella gave me the low warning growl of a mom on alert. I directed, "Spread some newspaper on your desk, and I'll examine her there, away from the pups." I took her temperature first. It was possible some placenta had been retained, which would cause a low-grade infection and be a possible cause of her symptoms. Yet the other vet had said she was afebrile, and there was still no fever. I palpated her abdomen, and the uterus had involuted normally and was the size it should be. Everything checked out okay. Her mammary glands, while not as full as I wished, were still providing milk.

Stella was not afraid of or resentful of my exam. She was still and quiet, and showed her appreciation of my several pats and conversation with an occasional wag of her docked tail. She obviously received much affection from her now-crooning owner, and she had the manner of a well-disciplined but adored pet.

Mentally I ran through what abnormalities could produce this picture. Mr. De Cavalante was right, she was too thin and dispirited, especially for a bouncy terrier—even one who was nursing. And just a cursory look at the pups revealed under-development. I was stymied, but not for long.

Stella began a faint trembling, a twitching of various groups of muscles. "See, that's what I mean," Mr. De Cavalante said. It was the tip-off. What the hell was wrong with me! I should have been thinking eclampsia right along! I had, over the years, seen a couple of sub-clinical postpartum eclampsia cases exactly like Stella's. In the full-blown cases of eclampsia (known as milk fever in cows), the bitch would collapse, convulse, and if unattended, could die. The cause was low blood calcium. In rare cases, the demands of producing milk were too much for the bitch. It was not always a dietary deficiency of calcium, although that was a possibility. Stella, of course, had a completely balanced diet—the best.

While I would have preferred to do blood work to confirm my diagnosis, it wasn't really necessary. I took a syringe, filled it with the proper amount of calcium gluconate, and slowly administered it intravenously. The results would verify my diagnosis, if it was correct. If not, no harm done. I have seen cows collapsed with milk fever get on their feet and start grazing shortly after the calcium injection. If Stella ceased the muscle twitching and trembling, I'd be on target.

My Irish luck and previous experience won the day. Mr. De Cavalante was overjoyed when I explained the situation and that all would be well. He couldn't have been happier if Stella had been an actual daughter.

I was ready for the certain question: "Dr. Scanlon, how come my vet didn't diagnose it? It seems so simple and logical the way you explain it."

I casually explained, "He didn't have the advantage of seeing the eclampsia-like seizure like I did. Now I'll call him and he will monitor Stella and care for her, exactly as I would." Like physicians, we vets try to cover one another's butts. One never knows, someday the shoe could be on the other foot. In cases of negligence, though, we never cover.

"The Don," as I now think of him, was too gentlemanly to offer payment. He gave me his card. It said "New Hope Investment and Realty Management, Inc." He said, "Please bill me and remember how much I appreciate your help."

I did. His check arrived promptly, with a handwritten note: "I have instructed Silvio that on as many occasions as you wish, you and yours are to be my guests at his restaurant. My sincerest gratitude, and Stella's regards."

Consorting with the mob? I suppose I was guilty. Especially when one of my daughters graduated, and when another wed. Silvio's free meals were equally relished on birthdays and anniversaries. Thankfully, he never asked for another "favor."

Years later, reading about The Don's trial in federal court was fascinating to me. How did a man, bright and educated, go wrong? It seems his parents had emigrated from Italy when he was young. Since he was bilingual and a graduate lawyer, most of his clients were of Italian descent, and many were mobsters. Being very intelligent, he decided, at one point, to take over. Why advise them when he could better manage their businesses and rackets? Like the recent "Teflon Don," John Gotti, he was betrayed by his underlings. Omerta, the code of silence, was forgotten when they faced jail.

I prefer to think of him as a loving grandfather and Stella's doting owner.

thirteen

Another Fortune Lost

"Hello, Mr. Hanson?"

"Yes, speaking."

"I'm a harness horse person and I saw your full-page ad for the AQUA-CISER in *Harness Horse* magazine this week. It seems like a wonderful invention and I'm interested." It had been a two-page spread and very visible.

Mr. David Hanson of Chicago, the advertised president and CEO of AQUA-CISER, Inc., proceeded to extol the miraculous effects the AQUA-CISER would produce for racehorses. "It will prevent lameness and is a wonderful healing tool for those already lame or sore. It will enhance their strength and speed. It is making winners out of previous losers." It sounded like a well-rehearsed sales pitch, and just its beginning.

I interrupted. "I notice you have the AQUA-CISER name trademarked, but no patent."

"Well, that's in the works. It will be patented shortly."

"You're a liar, Mr. Hanson," I said with a little heat.

"A liar? What do you mean?"

"I mean you aren't telling the truth. This is Dr. Edward Scanlon, and you know damn well I hold the patent on it. When your attorney checked, you were bound to find out it was issued to me."

"Uh-huh, well . . ."

"Skip the uh-huhs. Why didn't you call me? You know you're in violation of my patent rights." More steam was building up. "I know you're a liar, and, I suspect, a thief."

"Now hold on, Dr. Scanlon. I'm only following my lawyer's advice."

"Which was?"

"Well, first off, he said you might be dead. You've had the patent for over a year with no attempt to manufacture or sell the product. Maybe if you were dead your estate might not be aware of your patent. Then, if you were alive or they were aware, someone would get in touch, which you have. We're very willing to negotiate a fair deal. I have no intention of cheating you or anyone."

Our conversation ended with a date to meet three days later at the small Chester County airport, the closest to me. Hanson, it turned out, was an amateur pilot, as well as an engineer and a sulky horseman. He also owned, trained, and raced horses at the big Chicago-area tracks. My evaluation of him improved slightly. Still, I knew he could easily have contacted me, and it isn't often you talk to someone who has the audacity to tell you he would have benefited from your death. My last words to him were, "Be sure to bring money."

What was the AQUA-CISER and whence had it come? Very simply, it was a fiberglass chamber to contain fluids (usually water), with Jacuzzi-like jets in the walls and a treadmill on the floor. It had other accessories like a heater and a pump to empty and fill the chamber, plus an underground water storage tank. The temperature of the fluid could be hot, tepid, or cold, depending on the requirements of training or injury. The temperature and jet action were therapeutic for soreness or lameness in the horse (or human, for that matter). The variable treadmill speed provided muscle, lung, and heart conditioning with minimal concussion and trauma to the limbs, as opposed to conditioning on a hard racetrack.

The buoyancy of the water took considerable weight off the horse's fragile legs. Thus, a racehorse could be conditioned with minimal trauma, and various leg ailments could be helped or cured while the horse maintained racing condition. One problem with horses, as with any other athlete, is that they lose their racing edge while they're healing and have to begin training to build strength, endurance, and speed all over again.

The AQUA-CISER came into being because my cousin and horse partner, Dan O'Neill, and I were appalled at the lameness we encountered in the sport. It seemed one of our horses was always recovering from an injury, and our friends were suffering the same complaints. Our injured horses often had to be sold for riding or to the Amish as buggy horses, because they couldn't race. Our conclusion was that the daily concussion of the fragile legs on the hard track during the training and conditioning process was largely responsible. There are, of course, many other causes of lameness, including faulty confirmation (such as crooked legs), but we felt that less trauma had to help in the prevention of lameness.

We harness horse owners weren't alone in these problems. The 1996 Kentucky Derby winner, Grindstone, went lame the week after his victory. Instead of going on to the other two jewels of the Triple Crown, he went on to retirement. His extraordinary racing career was over.

Our answer to reducing trauma was the AQUA-CISER: keep horses off the track except when racing or learning necessary manners and education. Some trainers conditioned their horses in a swimming pool or lake with excellent results. But for the average horseman, a pool was too expensive and few had access to ponds or lakes. The AQUA-CISER would make water conditioning available to all.

The concept of the machine seemed too simple, so I never

thought it would be patentable. However, a patent attorney who was also a client agreed to investigate. He assured me after a preliminary search that such an apparatus had never been patented, so we applied for one. The U.S. Patent Office granted me patent #3485213 on the AQUA-CISER, to my surprise and pleasure. I thought of Dr. Stader, my mentor and friend. As an inventor himself, he would have been proud of me.

Dave Hanson's plane was on time. We met on the tarmac of the airport, as agreed. His previously described small bird was the only one in sight. The man who emerged was a well-dressed, average-looking person with a strong handshake and an enthusiastic manner. He appeared to be in his mid-thirties. He looked me directly in the eye and started out with a compliment. "Great minds run in the same channel, but you were ahead of me on the AQUA-CISER concept."

He was, it seemed, a good salesman. "No hard feelings, Doc," with a pat on my back. "Our interests are mutual. Forgive my stupidity in following my dumb lawyer's advice. I should have called you right at the start." I agreed.

We repaired to a good local restaurant for dinner and, more important, negotiations hopefully leading to an agreement. After much give-and-take, we finally agreed on a $10,000 fee to me for transferring the patent rights to his corporation. I was to receive a 4 percent royalty on each unit sold. Since my lawyer had advised that 2 percent to 3 percent was usual, I was willing to back down from my original requirement of $15,000 for transfer rights. I believed the results the AQUA-CISER could achieve would make it a good seller. Since Dan and I were too busy and lacked the capital to manufacture and promote the apparatus, I was willing to trade some up-front money for a bigger royalty. Besides, at that point we had no horses racing, and were concentrating on breeding a few mares. We were planning to sell the patent at a future time, although we had made no efforts in that direction so far. Maybe Hanson would be just what we needed to capitalize on our idea.

He was to pay the royalty each quarter with a complete

sales report and access to his books on request. I asked about sales, as I hoped to have some royalty money already accruing. The agreement was to be retroactive. "How many units have you sold to date?"

Hanson explained that he had sold only one, at cost, to a California veterinarian who was treating the movie-star horse from *The Black Stallion*. The horse was recovering nicely, and Hanson had a videotape of the animal in the apparatus. He felt it would be an invaluable promotional tool. "I'll show it to you tomorrow," he promised. "Doc, you caught my first advertisement, and it has drawn a lot of interest. We'll be closing a lot of sales very soon."

He had made arrangements to stay overnight and, if we could reach an agreement, have it finalized and signed in my attorney's office. We agreed to meet and do the deal in the morning.

At signing time, he raised "just one little problem." He could pay only $5,000 then, but would sign a promissory note for the balance, due in three months. He explained that his advertising and start-up costs were heavy, which was understandable. His enthusiasm was contagious, but I didn't like receiving only half of the front money. A few doubts lingered, but the Black Stallion tape, plus his other sales pitch, prevailed. I signed.

The tape opened with Hanson, against a gorgeous blue California sky, describing the AQUA-CISER. The Black Stallion, an awe-inspiring, coal-black animal, was shown in the equipment at a fast walk. His shoulder injury, fence-incurred, was described as healing many times faster than with ordinary therapy. Hanson ended with something like, "Thanks to the AQUA-CISER, he will resume his career and star in new movies. He will again be able to thrill adults and children with his free, flowing motion." The tape was professional and quite impressive.

On reflection, Hanson was heaven-sent. He was an engineer, an articulate salesman, enthusiastic about the product (*my* product) and after all, he had to have invested considerable personal money to have come this far. He professed to have a first-class manufacturing plant lined up to build the units. He seemed to be the ideal person to promote and sell my invention. Lady Luck was smiling on me.

Hanson enthused, "Just wait till we get into production on the smaller, less expensive human model. Every hospital, rehab center, every health club and spa in the country will need one or two." Yes indeed, Dave Hanson was my man. Although I was becoming comfortable financially, the thoughts of my coming wealth were heady. The security I could give my wife and children, the college funds that could be established for my hoped-for grandchildren, the many luxuries I could afford were somewhat intoxicating.

It looked like a "can't miss" situation. The human fitness apparatus market was just beginning to emerge. People were watching their diets, exercising fanatically. I agreed with Hanson that the racehorse market was limited but that the human model's market was boundless. Still, I remembered Grandma's admonition "Don't count the chicks till they hatch." But it looked for sure like there would be a lot of eggs. I envisioned the huge royalty checks coming in every quarter. How could it miss? I had forgotten the Stader Splint and Murphy's Law. How right Grandma was.

I received the final $5,000 only after many threats from my lawyer, and never a cent of royalty fees. I knew Hanson had sold a small number of horse units to some racetracks and one to a big training farm in New Jersey. Yet his quarterly reports, proffered only after more legal threats, showed no sales at all. After almost a year of legal fighting for non-payment of royalties, my attorney sued for breach of contract and recovered the patent rights. My legal fees had eaten up most of the last $5,000 payment from Hanson. My dreams of riches were evaporating and finally expired.

I advertised and attempted to resell the patent. My efforts were futile since Hanson had gone bankrupt; a number of his units were faulty and resulted in several lawsuits. The name

AQUA-CISER—which I had dreamt would be a famous one, attached to a helpful medical and conditioning invention—was in disrepute.

Fortunately, I had not spent any of the dreamt-of fortune. Grandma's advice again: "Don't spend it till you get it." Old-fashioned, but wise.

At this point, I was fed up with the AQUA-CISER. I disposed of it by presenting the patent rights to my alma mater, the University of Pennsylvania's veterinary school. They were enthused about its prospects in animal healing and conditioning and were eagerly awaiting the time when they could raise the funds to further its use. But no such funds appeared. The patent lay in some professor's desk drawer and finally expired there when its eighteen-year life span ran out. I didn't mourn its death. It had long been forgotten.

I was able to take a tax deduction for the gift on my year-end return, and that probably just about put me in the financial "plus" column. I had no real complaints, though: my practice was flourishing and at that point employed three full-time veterinarians. For a time, it had been fun to daydream about riches, and see myself as the Henry Ford–like pioneer of training and conditioning apparatus.

Live and learn. I did learn that a patent affords little protection in some cases. In fact, with some changes, it can be a blueprint, a diagram for imitators. Not long after the AQUA-CISER's appearance, several large companies produced their own versions of the apparatus. Some appeared, according to my attorney, to be in violation of mine. I had no stomach for a fight, nor would I commit any more funds to pursue them. The AQUA-CISER was fun for a while. In the end, it was an aspirin-proof headache.

Dan and I still have the original experimental model. Through the years it has helped some of our sore horses and it has even provided us with a few laughs over our "lost millions." As racehorse people have said a thousand times, you can't win them all.

fourteen

Take a Stand

All veterinarians have to take a position on animal experimentation. This isn't as easy as it might seem: On the one hand, their lives are devoted to caring for animals, but on the other hand there's their role as scientists. This is a touchy subject. The proliferation of animal activists who equate animals' rights with humans' has been phenomenal in my lifetime. They are dedicated to their cause, and they have raised public awareness of the need to protect all animals. For that, they deserve credit. Unfortunately, some of these activists are zealots who have wrecked some important research projects and labs. There is much to be argued on both sides. The pro-rights contend there should be no animals used in research. Many scientists argue that without animal use, medical progress would be severely curtailed.

I arrived at my position during the time before a vaccine for polio was found. My youngest daughters were toddlers when polio was a scourge. Schools and public pools and parks

closed during polio outbreaks because of the high rate of con-
tagion. Parents' hearts froze when a child ran a fever. Families were shattered when beloved children became paralyzed
and too often spent the rest of their shortened lives in iron
lungs. People today can't begin to understand the fear and
devastation this disease brought. No one was immune.

Today, vaccines are taken for granted. My mother died in
a flu epidemic that wiped out one in ten people in our nation;
now there is a vaccine people use routinely. The vaccines we
administer so casually today, the vaccines that have eradicated not only disease but true fear, were all, each and every
one, made possible by animal experimentation.

Diseases that currently are killers—cancer, AIDS, and di-
abetes come to mind—will eventually be eradicated. But it
will not happen without some animal experimentation. To be
against all animal testing is to deny ourselves and our children protection and to postpone disease eradication. Small-
pox no longer exists. The former plague succumbed to vaccination, as will some current diseases.

With that said, I must add that I believe much animal experimentation is immoral and unnecessary. Why should a
bunny's eyes be stitched open to see how they respond to hair
spray as a possible irritant? The hair spray formula contains,
for example, alcohol. It's already well known that alcohol is an
eye irritant. To put a rabbit through that is inexcusable. Cos-
metics and beauty aids are not essential, and their absence
isn't life-threatening.

If it has been determined that an experiment's results are
vital in the quest for important knowledge, then the animal
must be treated as humanely as possible, before, during, and
after the experiment, with pain control being of paramount
importance. To do otherwise is to betray our own humanity.
We vets, and all medical researchers, must give more thought
and effort to the protection of laboratory animals and the quality of their care. It is vital that the approach called "best of
care only" be continued and improved.

My very limited participation in the use of animals in research caused me to do some intense soul-searching and left me both sad and elated. My first such experience was during my internship with Dr. Stader. We were doing the field work—testing—on a new distemper vaccine developed by his close colleague Dr. Green, who had been commissioned by the American Mink Breeders Association to produce a vaccine. The virus was decimating that industry. Dr. Green was delighted to do this, since the need in dogs was even greater. Most people aren't old enough to remember how adored pets died miserably with this disease; many survivors were brain-damaged or handicapped.

Dr. Green had passed the virus through a number of generations of live ferrets and believed it was attenuated (weakened) to the extent that it would not cause disease. The question now was whether it would still have enough life to stimulate the dogs' or minks' immune systems against the distemper virus. In the development of any live vaccine, there is a very narrow line between disease-causing and disease-preventing, and it must be animal-tested to find the right balance. It is the only way to determine the correct dosage and discover any side effects.

We kept a small, isolated colony of young dogs in a large separate garage near the Ardmore Animal Hospital. We vaccinated at first with 5 milligrams of Dr. Green's vaccine, and then exposed the dogs to the live virus. They all contracted distemper and had to be euthanized. Dr. Stader then upped the dose to 20 milligrams. He explained we were working with the "cell block" theory, which was new at the time. Basically, it says that if we get our "good stuff" into the cells, that leaves no room for the "bad stuff." I had my doubts, but at the increased dosage, only about half the dogs contracted the disease and had to be euthanized.

Finally, at 75 milligrams, all the dogs withstood a live virus challenge. No distemper; they were immune! Hallelujah! We saw the light and were out of the tunnel of darkness.

Dr. Stader was elated. "We've done it, Dr. Scanlon. Finally."

I, too, was joyful because we at last had an effective weapon against distemper. To be part of this salvation for animals, and I do not use the word *salvation* loosely, was a landmark in my life and career. But I was also mindful that we had caused disease in healthy, young dogs and then killed them. I found that very difficult; the isolated dogs were so trusting and eager for my company. I fed, exercised, and walked them daily. I had grown attached despite my efforts not to. I knew each one.

I expressed myself to my mentor. "Yes," he said, "we killed some dogs. But how many hundreds of thousands of dogs will we save?" For once he was patient and understanding of my feelings.

"Look at it this way, Dr. Scanlon. We have been fighting a war with distemper as long as there has been veterinary medicine. And we've been losing, never won even a single battle. We're fighting a war against disease and in war, you lose soldiers. Those dogs were heroes, just like the boys dying in battle right now." His tone softened. "Do you think I enjoyed that part? Do you think any vet does? It never gets better, and if you get so you don't mind it, then get out of the profession."

His analogy did cheer me somewhat, but I still felt guilty. My guilt was gradually alleviated as the so-called Green Vaccine was hailed as the savior of the mink industry (which moved me very little) and chiefly as a boon to the canine world.

My other experience with field testing, of another canine distemper vaccine, came a few years later, when I was in practice. It was all pleasure, no pain. No lost soldiers!

Dr. Hilary Kaprowski, later head of the famed Wistar Institute at the University of Pennsylvania, had approached the distemper prevention problem in an entirely different way than Dr. Green had. He had brilliantly attenuated the virus on fertilized chicken eggs. After many passages, it had great

immune-producing powers and no capacity to produce the Animal
disease. And what's cheaper than chicken eggs? They were Patients
certainly less expensive than ferrets! It was called Avianized
Distemper Vaccine, after the chicken, and so trademarked by
Lederle Labs.

Dr. Kaprowski approached me to help with the final field
testing. The bait for my work and participation was that after
successful testing, my name would appear on the published
report along with Dr. Kaprowski's name. I was also to receive
free vaccine for two years after the field work. I would have to
keep meticulous records, and I had Dr. Kaprowski's assur-
ance that the vaccine had proven perfect, with no side effects,
in his laboratory tests.

It took me the better part of a year to test the vaccine because Lederle wanted results on at least one hundred dogs. It
was a great vaccine, without side effects of any kind. One-year
and two-year follow-up results were done, and proved the vaccine to be 98 percent effective. When the results were reported in the prestigious *Journal of Veterinary Medicine* with
my name as co-author, I was thrilled. Just about every veterinarian in the country read it cover to cover, and it was respected worldwide.

Of course, there are ethics that prevented me from using
an unlicensed, experimental vaccine on an unsuspecting
owner's pet. Ethics, both professional and personal, demanded that owners be advised. I told them that, in my opinion and that of the famous virologist, the vaccine was safe and
effective. It was also free; they paid only for the office call and
the examination. The available Green Vaccine was so expensive, I felt I was offering my pet owners a real bargain. Actually, it was used two to one by my more modest-income
clients. They were required to sign a consent form, which was
one reason the vaccine took so long to test. The mere word *experimental* was frightening to some owners, but we owed them
nothing less than complete honesty, and that's what they got.

My affiliation with Lederle Labs on the Avianized Distem-

163

per Vaccine field work brought me other benefits in later years. When they were developing new antibiotics, I again did some field work for them, to the benefit of many patients. The new drugs that I received were usually very expensive when they were first available. Because I received them for free, I was able to give my clients a break. The antibiotics had already undergone thorough and extensive testing, and my patients were often receiving antibiotics sooner than their human masters. Some of the drugs I tested, such as tetracycline, were miraculous.

Many veterinarians are employed by the large drug companies in research. I couldn't spend my education and time in such work, no matter how necessary; I needed the contact with the owners and hands-on work with patients. Yet as the saying goes, someone has to do it, and I for one am grateful for these vets' less glamorous and less financially rewarding work. Many have contributed to the discovery of today's miracle drugs.

Some of my other scientific articles were published and fairly well-received, including several about physical therapy in racehorses. Those articles were mostly about the AQUA-CISER. Another was about a kitten who was one of the most amazing cases I ever had. It had a condition called atresia anii, which means it had been born without an anal sphincter or orifice. I had seen a case of this before, but never an afflicted animal that had reached the age of six weeks. Astonishingly, it had lived that long without any bowel elimination. What an observant owner!

I am proudest of the publication of the field work I did in connection with the earliest successful canine distemper vaccines. A few years after they became available, the dreadful scourge began to abate, and now most veterinarians go a long time without seeing a case. Dr. Stader was right; our vaccine eventually saved millions of canine and mink lives. But I have never forgotten our twenty-five "soldiers" who gave their lives

for the cause.

About the use of mink and other animal skins for clothing: Sorry, but I think it's wrong. It perpetuates unnecessary cruel treatment of animals. So-called ranch-raised pelts come from caged, unnaturally raised animals. In terms of ethics, people pay too much for such apparel. All those beautiful, non-consenting animals are killed to cater to vanity. Synthetic or "fake" furs are just as warm and can be worn guilt-free. Like today's imitation diamonds, they are almost indistinguishable from the real thing, and they are not stained with blood. Please think about the real cost in animal suffering before you purchase furs.

fifteen

Surgeons, Fishmongers, and Whippets

What did a well-known Main Line surgeon and the area's best-known fishmonger have in common during the '60s and '70s? Whippets. Lots of whippets. Between them they had forty or more at any given time during that period.

The surgeon, Dr. Clare Hodge, had a keen interest in whippets and in breeding and showing them, but he didn't have much time to spend on his hobby. His wife, Peggy, an even stronger devotee and lover of the breed, handled the kennel chores. She supervised the travel, the showing, the breeding, and the daily care of their racy-looking breed. For those not familiar with this delightful animal, whippets are a medium-sized cousin of the greyhound. (The smallest greyhound is the Italian toy.)

The Hodges' kennel, predictably, was the finest that love and money could buy. Although they utilized other veterinarians' services on occasion, as I sometimes recommended a second opinion, I was privileged to attend to most of their dogs' medical and surgical needs over the years.

Dr. Hodge had a large, devoted following. He was a fine-featured, good-looking man, with prematurely snow-white hair that matched his strong, even, white teeth, which were frequently exposed in a great smile. In addition to his superior surgical skills, his "bedside manner" especially endeared him to his numerous patients. He repaired an inguinal hernia for me, so I experienced first hand his skill and charisma. I felt I was his only patient. He visited me every morning and again about 10:30 each evening, his usual practice.

Everyone marveled at the doctor's stamina. He believed that four to five hours' sleep was adequate for healthy people if they "trained" themselves. His eighteen-hour days and six-day weeks enabled him to handle a much larger caseload than an average surgeon. Bryn Mawr Hospital's surgical wing was always overflowing with his recuperating charges.

I could never understand, nor could most of his patients, why he was indicted for tax evasion. He was known for sending out bills six to eight months after the surgery. He never took a vacation, and he drove inexpensive cars. Like Dr. Stader, money, to him, seemed immaterial. He never did bill me or immediate family members for his surgeries.

Nevertheless, he was charged with tax evasion and pleaded no contest. The Main Line and Philadelphia were buzzing and gossiping for weeks prior to his trial. His defenders blamed his predicament on his bookkeepers, his wife, anyone but Dr. Hodge himself. The *Philadelphia Inquirer*'s daily headlines kept the pot boiling.

His numerous defenders actually hurt him when it came to the judge's sentence. Many a lesser-known offender would have received a large fine, probation, or a sixty-day sentence at most. Not Clare Hodge. The unhappy judge was besieged with letters, calls, petitions, telegrams, and personal pleas to spare the beloved physician jail time. Like they later did during the O.J. Simpson trial, the media speculated daily on the outcome. The bottom line was that the judge, because of the pressure and publicity, had to give Dr. Hodge a meaningful sentence. I seem to recall it was one to three years.

What a waste of talent. Well, not exactly. He plied his surgical skills, thanks to an enlightened warden, while "paying his debt to society." There were any number of prisoners who benefited from his talented scalpel who would otherwise have gone untreated. There were stories of cosmetic miracles as well as routine repairs. Even after his release, he returned to prison every month to contribute his services.

During his incarceration, I got to know and admire his wife, Peggy. She was positive, cheerful, and even humorous about the situation: "I see more of my husband in jail than I ever did." I sensed that the many dogs were a partial substitute for his absence and workaholic ways.

When he was released from jail, the board of directors at Bryn Mawr Hospital handed Dr. Hodge another blow. Despite his years of service there, and his having served his time, they voted to withdraw his hospital privileges. This caused more media headlines and storms of protest. Many people, including me, blasted this decision and withdrew their financial support of the hospital.

A surgeon without a hospital is useless, but Clare Hodge was happily embraced by a modest-sized Philadelphia hospital, St. Joseph's on Girard Avenue. He repaid the directors' faith in him by filling up the hospital with his adoring patients. In a sense, he put St. Joseph's on the map. Later Dr. Hodge became affiliated with the growing Main Line Hospital in Paoli and carried on his huge practice there for many years. Our friendship endured, and we had the pleasure of watching the friendship of his son and my daughter Martha while they were in high school together.

Roland Hill, Sr., purveyor through several outlets of the finest seafood on the Main Line, was another whippet lover, exhibitor, and breeder. Like the Hodges, he believed in numbers.

We first met when he presented me with a beautiful tan brindle show dog afflicted with oral papilloma—mouth and lip warts. They were large, numerous, unsightly, even repulsive. They caused the uncomfortable dog to salivate and lick his lips. "Can you believe my luck," he said. "He was scheduled to compete in five days at the Devon Dog Show." He shook his head. "No way I can show him now. What gives? I've been in dogs for years and never seen this."

I explained to Mr. Hill that it was indeed a rare condition, caused by a virus. "There isn't a lot known about it, but it does respond to treatment. In fact, I've had some dramatic results in just a few days in some cases," I told him cautiously.

"You mean you can clear this up in time for the show?" His voice was rising, a little excited. "That would be a miracle."

Mindful of my teachers' cautions that only quacks guaranteed results, I carefully responded, "I can't promise for sure, but I think we have a good chance of getting that blue ribbon. That's assuming he's as good as you claim." I couldn't resist teasing him a little. "You know, Mr. Hill, most every show person who brings me a dog assures me it is unbeatable."

He frowned a little. "Tell you what. You clear him up by show time, and I'll pay your fee gladly. If he doesn't win his class, I'll pay your fee double. If he does, you remit your fee to me."

I laughed, appreciating his line of thought. "No thanks! You sound too sure, and I'm not a gambling man." Thinking of my racehorses, I mentally called myself a liar.

"The treatment," I offered, returning to his question, "consists of surgical excising of the biggest warts and the injection of a wart vaccine. I'll keep him overnight because he will have to have anesthesia."

The minute Mr. Hill left, I was on the phone to procure a new vial of the wart vaccine. I had so little use for it that the one I had was outdated. The results of my therapy were amazing, even to me. In three days, the lips, tongue, and oral cavity of the little beauty were completely normal. I could read the relief from discomfort in his moist, dark eyes, which gave me more of a payoff than winning a bet ever could.

Mr. Hill was delighted with the results. "Great work! Peggy Hodge is going to be sorry she referred me to you. My Paradigm is going to shame her top dogs. We'll win without a doubt. How about that bet? Why don't you take me up on it?" He was on a high.

"No thanks, Mr. Hill. Having had a chance to study him and get to know him, I agree. He could be unbeatable."

He was.

Mr. Hill and I got along just fine for a time. I enjoyed participating in his dogs' care. It all ended when fourteen dewclaws caused an abrupt parting.

A dewclaw is a superfluous appendage on the lower inner side of a dog's front leg, sort of a vestigial toe with a claw. An inch or so above the paws, it has no contact with the ground and just keeps growing. Dewclaws frequently become torn and infected when caught on grasses until they are removed.

Their removal is simple and painless and heals quickly when it's done at two to four days of age. When the pups are born, the dewclaws are a very soft cartilage that becomes progressively harder until it turns to bone by five or six weeks. Then they are painful and difficult to remove and heal slowly, with a higher level of possible infection. The standard of many breeds calls for the removal of dewclaws. The whippet is such a breed.

Mr. Hill turned up one day with seven pups, six weeks of age. "They need their shots and the dewclaws removed."

I proceeded to berate him. "You know darn well they should have been removed at two days, while they were soft. Either this is negligence, or you just don't give a damn about their pain." I was disgusted and threw up my hands.

His face turned red. "I didn't come here to get a lecture. You know the Yellow Pages are full of people like you."

Exit Mr. Hill and fourteen dewclaws. I didn't miss Hill, but I did miss his dogs. They were cheerful little animals, with

great heart and spirit, and were uniformly handsome and of
top show quality.

Later in my career, I had an opportunity for a pleasing and
educational association with another great Philadelphia surgeon. Dr. Anthony De Palma was well known for his orthopedic miracles and later for a talented son. He was the father of
movie director Brian De Palma.

I treated Dr. De Palma's household pets, but my closest association had to do with his experimental dogs. He was chief
of orthopedic surgery at Jefferson Medical College. Among his
numerous missions was to solve the problems encountered in
healing children's broken bones.

Adults' bones have stopped growing, while children's are
still changing and represent a different challenge. To try to get
some answers, Dr. De Palma kept a research colony of growing young pups in his laboratory. He encountered a number of
health problems and diseases with them that in some cases
nullified or obscured months of his work and hopes.

He called me in and said simply (like Dr. Stader, no please
or thanks), "Take over, I can't have these problems."

He did add, "The pay will be minimal, as our budget is
small." Shades of the SPCA's CEO. Still, the prospect of working with and learning from a person of his stature was exhila-
rating. "No problem, Dr. De Palma. I'll be happy if you just
cover my expenses and drugs." That was our agreement.

It was a great experience, despite my disappointment at
seeing very little of the great orthopedist. I worked mostly
with his second-in-command, a Dr. Wolfington. It was stimulating to mingle with these top surgeons and the chiefs of various other specialties.

I started with the basics. The dogs' nutritional program
was poor and erratic. The worming and vaccination schedules
were haphazard at best. I stopped the practice of bringing new
dogs into the colony without first isolating them to be sure
they were disease-free. The problem was simply that no one
was in charge. I hired an intelligent, reliable, eager man,

stolen from the SPCA, to supervise. In about six months, the dogs' health problems all but disappeared.

Dr. De Palma was pleased and did thank me. "I'll stop by every couple of weeks to check on things. Gratis, of course," I assured him. I wasn't going to miss out completely on those great lunches and intellectual banquets with Wolfington.

Dr. De Palma was thoughtful enough to send me a copy of his research paper. He came up with some important new findings and techniques for solving the problems of fractures in children, and many children today benefit from this seminal research. The publication was authored by De Palma, Wolfington, and several other associates. My name didn't appear. My gratification was knowing I had made a small contribution to this important work.

sixteen

On the State Board

As I said before, Dr. Stader eventually sold the Ardmore Animal Hospital (which is how I acquired the services of the incomparable Mrs. Walsh) and retired. For him, retirement didn't mean quite the same thing it did for other people. He was active with referral surgeries, which he performed at the requesting veterinarian's hospital, and with numerous business initiatives and travel. The heavens only knew what inventions he had in the works.

One day his part-time secretary phoned. "Dr. Scanlon? Dr. Stader will be with you momentarily." It was a long "momentarily," and when he finally came on, it was a vintage Stader conversation: no "good morning," no "how are you," even though we hadn't talked in a while. Straight to the point.

"How would you like to be the youngest vet ever appointed to the Pennsylvania State Board of Veterinary Medical Examiners?"

Quickly, I mentally reviewed what I knew about the organization. There were three members, appointed by the state's governor and approved by the state senate. They were a body with the power to examine and license veterinarians who were working or practicing in the state. They could also revoke a license if sufficient evidence of malpractice or "unprofessional conduct" (a purposely broad term) was brought before them. They also prosecuted (through the attorney general's office) anyone practicing medicine or surgery without a license. They had other powers, but those were the essential three.

No one sought the office for monetary reasons. There was a small per diem payment—a skimpy allowance for mileage and meals. It was perceived as a prestigious appointment, often equated with high professional ability. That was untrue. It was strictly a political appointment, but it was considered an honor, a chance to serve and to give something back to veterinary medicine.

Dr. Stader continued, "I am about to resign my appointment, and I have the connections to have you appointed as my replacement, if you are interested." That he did, no question. With his endorsement, it would be a done deal. I paused. There was, I knew, something else involved. As soon as I said "It would be an honor to serve on the board," it surfaced. "Dr. Scanlon, I know you can and will do a good job. I would be counting on you to continue pressing for my internship program."

His proposed plan was controversial and was before the board for study. It had not yet been passed into law, but would soon be voted on. The plan had been discussed in our professional journals, and its passage would be a landmark event. No other state had such a law.

Essentially, Stader proposed that it become mandatory that all new graduates serve a six-month internship with an approved, experienced vet after passing the state board exams but before formal licensure. His proponents claimed it would elevate the profession in the public mind, just like M.D.'s, who all served an internship. It would also ensure practical experience and learning before hanging out one's shingle.

Opponents argued that, practically speaking, everyone did an internship anyway. They claimed it would place new graduates in a position of dependency on their employer. The preceptor could, in effect, pay low wages and demand more work. Since the experienced vet would call the tune, the new graduate could be a slave in actuality, if not in name.

Having been an "intern" under Dr. Stader during my senior year in vet school, and having experienced his ideas on compensation and work hours, I leaned toward the new graduates' view. They were all against his mandatory internship program.

"Can't you continue for a while?" I temporized. "No one can promote it like you."

"Ed" (At that, I almost dropped the phone. He had never used my first name before), "I have serious coronary problems. I have to step down now." His tone made it impossible for me to ask further questions, although my concern for my old mentor, friend, and idol crowded out my interest in the position.

I was no longer a raw graduate and had learned a little about the "noncommittal but encouraging" answer. "Dr. Stader, if appointed, I would give considerable thought and study to your proposal. It certainly is very interesting. I'm just not familiar enough with the details to make a judgment at this moment." Translated, no promises, but I'd love the job. It would belittle my relationship with—and my respect for—him to give him false answers just because of his illness.

"Fair enough. I have confidence in your judgment. I'm going to recommend your appointment." No good-bye, just a phone click.

About two weeks later, I began to receive some congratulatory phone calls from friends and clients on my appointment to the board. The Philadelphia newspapers had announced the prominent Dr. Stader's resignation and my appointment by the governor as his replacement. The conclusion could be drawn that I was in his class; no way possible, but the announcement did bring in some impressed new clients.

My first board meeting was held in the capital city of Harrisburg. I enjoyed the drive from my hospital to those meetings. It was about a two-hour trip, through some beautiful Pennsylvania countryside. It was peaceful (no car phones or beepers back in that day), and the picture-perfect farms, barns, and grazing dairy cows and horses provided a fresh perspective.

My respect for and understanding of large-animal veterinarians increased. They spent a lot of time driving to and from those farms, servicing the dairy industry, the turkey and chicken farms, and the hog and sheep raisers. It was easier to understand their feelings toward us small-animal practitioners. Many of them felt they were serving the real needs of the animal world, and they often considered the small-animal vets to be catering to the frivolous aspects of the profession.

What a wonderful profession I was part of. Regardless of one's animal preference, we managed to give quality medical and surgical attention to, as James Herriot put it, all creatures great and small.

Our board met in the large offices of professional licensure. The barbers' and hairdressers' licensure had adjacent offices. The chairman of our board, Dr. Lee, and his associate Dr. Orcutt welcomed me and congratulated me on my appointment before we sat down for business.

My fellow board members were a study in contrast. Dr. Orcutt was a bovine specialist and one of those vets who considered small-animal practice to be rather effete. Looking at him, you could understand how he fit his job. He was an oversized man, at least six feet three inches tall, with strong, large hands. His face was weather-beaten from working in pastures and barnyards. I could visualize him in neat coveralls and sanitized rubber boots, tackling a recalcitrant calf. He was serious by nature, but enjoyed an occasional barnyard joke.

Dr. Lee was about five foot ten, and his appearance fit his Oriental name. He was far from inscrutable, though, and was a particularly funny man who made our sessions lively with his sense of the absurd and his willingness to see five sides of a question where an average person would see only three.

The board had the full-time services of a gracious and competent longtime secretary, Mrs. Francis. She really ran the show, as she had been there through many, many board members. She arranged the agenda and posted us on all important and trivial events, dates for future meetings, and examination dates. We submitted our vouchers for her approval, and only then were we paid.

At our first meeting, I became aware of the board's power regarding licensure. We were studying the results of our investigators' reports. The first complaint was against a vet in Delaware County, adjacent to my own Montgomery County. I knew him slightly. From the investigator's evidence, it appeared he was working a money-making scam on selected cases of mild digestive upsets in dogs.

Although fully aware that an animal brought to his office was not in serious condition, he would suggest that the problem just might be caused by a foreign body in the patient's digestive tract. To be sure, he would take a free X-ray. That, of course, suggested to the owner how caring and thorough he was. The rascal would insert an open safety pin between the animal's abdomen and the X-ray plate. The client's untrained eyes would plainly see the problem, a safety pin in the pet's stomach.

The charlatan had thus converted a mild, non-threatening digestive problem into a surgical emergency. The proper treatment, we all agreed, would have been to check for worms, put the pet on a binding diet, dispense an anti-emetic, give a mild anti-diarrhea compound, and have the owner check back in two days. A one-visit fee, two at most. Instead, the surgery necessary to remove the pin and the post-operative hospital care generated a very large fee.

The happy owner was grateful that his pet's life had been saved, and probably paid an inflated bill and spread the word about his "so competent" vet. Some owners were somewhat puzzled as to the source of the pin, though. "We don't have any loose safety pins around our house," one client later told our investigator. "We explained to the doctor that they are all kept away because of our baby, but he said it was probably in the grass or bushes. 'You know how they love to sniff and explore,' he told us."

The board now had to determine what punishment the quack should receive, since there was no question of his guilt. I was curious. "How did the board find out about this, and verify it was a scam?" I asked.

It seemed that about eighteen months after a safety pin episode, one of the dogs actually had a large bone lodged in his intestines, which was diagnosed by another vet when the emergency occurred during the con artist's vacation. The substitute vet was advised of the safety pin matter and the previous surgery. The vet was surprised and then angered when he found there had been only a skin incision made in the earlier surgery. There was no sign of abdominal cavity invasion. He was so upset he filed a complaint to the board. Our investigator had requested a look at the X-rays with the safety pin in the stomach, but they had somehow become lost. The investigator put some pressure on the suspected offender, and he confessed.

Dr. Lee, the chairman, queried, "Well, what punishment should we give him?"

Dr. Orcutt responded, "We could subpoena him for next month's meeting, since he's entitled to a lawyer. But I think that can be avoided if we give him a six-month license suspension. That should cure him."

Dr. Lee agreed. "We don't have any other cases or complaints against him." He turned to me. "Dr. Scanlon, you'll find that when they are caught doing it once, they have done it before." He picked up his pen. "What do you think? Six-month suspension from practice?"

It seemed fair to me, and Mrs. Francis concurred.

"So be it." Dr. Lee scribbled on the file. "You'll attend to

this, Mrs. Francis." Dr. Orcutt was shuffling papers and mut-
tering, "Reprehensible. Except for the fact that he has several
children, I'd have proposed a year's revocation of his license."

The next order of business was the status of some uncom-
pleted investigations of quacks, people who treated animals
for money without a state license to practice.

Dr. Lee advised, "The next case, that of Dr. Jenny, is a
painful one. We are all going to come out shit-covered and
with enemies in high places."

Shit-covered? Enemies in high places? I didn't remember
Dr. Stader including this in my job description. I listened
closely. All I knew was that Dr. Jenny was a teacher and a
highly skilled orthopedic surgeon and researcher at the University of Pennsylvania's veterinary school. He was a protégé
of the dean, Dr. Allam.

The problem was simple: He had no license to practice in
Pennsylvania. "Now, as long as Jenny worked under the surgical department's head and received a salary, we had no
problem. But we've been made aware that he's been accepting
referrals and taking fees. These charges are made by jealous
troublemakers, but we have to act on them."

I was puzzled. "How come a man of such talent doesn't
have a license?"

Dr. Lee was frustrated. "Pure bull. Red tape. He's a graduate of an unapproved school in Switzerland. Under our Pennsylvania act, only graduates of approved schools can take the
state board exams." He was becoming agitated. "Everyone's
pissed at us. The dean and many others are making us the
goats. The pressure has been terrible. What do you think, Dr.
Scanlon?"

"What are our options?" I asked.

"None. If we cave in, we violate our oaths to uphold the
veterinary act, which is very clear."

I suggested that the school award him an honorary degree.
Then he could be licensed.

"No soap, too complicated."

Edward J.
Scanlon

The board, with me concurring, took the cowardly way out. We postponed a decision. "Further study is needed." It was a mess. A truly outstanding vet and we couldn't legitimize him. We were accused of personal animosity toward Dr. Jenny, of holding out for a payoff, and of just being bastards. Jenny was very popular and accomplished, with many social friends.

At one of our meetings, I was startled to learn that one of my close neighboring colleagues had been under investigation. His problem was sexually based. At all of our meetings and seminars, he had always seemed to me to be pleasant, knowledgeable, and well-adjusted. In fact, he was generally well-liked and respected. He devoted time to and served on some state veterinary committees. But a number of complaints had been received from former female clients.

The tapeworm is a common parasite that can grow to a foot in length. The flea is the intermediate host, transferring the worm egg when a dog or cat ingests it. Dogs with tapeworms pass live, moist segments in the stool. These can also adhere about the anal region and appear like rice grains. Our problem colleague would point out the segments to the owner and tell her the parasite was frequently transferred to humans. He would then advise that he was more capable than an M.D. of diagnosing the condition in humans and would offer, as a courtesy, to examine the client, who was always a female. A proper examination, he would explain, necessitated her stripping and exposing her anal area. He would then massage the woman's buttocks and suggest he should go further.

Our investigator had the testimony of two women who had accepted this veterinarian's gratuitous services before realizing they had been duped. Both were courageously willing to face him personally. We felt their notarized and sworn depositions were adequate; no need to embarrass them further. No doubt there were unknown victims. It took courage for these women to admit their naiveté.

When the vet was formally charged at a hearing, his attorney pleaded *nolo contendre.* No contest; actually an admission of guilt. Deciding on his punishment was difficult. His tearful pleadings not to revoke his license were touching. "It would devastate my wife, my family, my livelihood. I'll never do it again. Never, never."

Thank God for our own Solomon, Dr. Lee. After consulting with the board, he pronounced judgment. "You deserve to lose your license, but if you go to the women you abused and humbly apologize and agree to psychiatric counseling for a year, furnishing them and the board with the monthly evidence of such treatment, then we will take no punitive action." He paused. "You are sick. They were demeaned and badly hurt. If they agree, there will be no revocation of license. If they aren't satisfied, since they are the injured parties, then you will lose your license. They will be your judges." I was very relieved. The judgment was fair. The doctor was allowed to continue to practice, thanks to the compassion of his victims.

I suspected we might hear about him again. A serious sexual sickness rooted in the psyche is not easily cured by counseling. It is "hard-wired" into the brain. I was right. He did eventually lose his license, several years after my second term expired. A very sad case.

The fun of being a board member was in giving and grading new graduates' exams for licensure. In most cases, it was a formality. Four years of college followed by four years of study at one of the finest vet schools in the world found them well prepared.

The board devised the questions on the many subjects and graded the applicants' answers. In some subjects, we required an oral exam and proof of manual dexterity. Rarely did a new graduate flunk. That wasn't true of some older vets, who had to take the exams if they moved into Pennsylvania from other states. They were often rusty on theory, though well versed in the practical aspects of their profession.

After my first year on the board, a new governor was elected. He was another Republican, and my reappointment was assured, as were those of Drs. Lee and Orcutt. Apparently any colleagues seeking our jobs lacked sufficient political connections to unseat us.

Despite the sometimes painful punishments we had to inflict on our erring professional brothers, I was glad to have the job. It gave me a chance to visit my cousin, Dan O'Neill, in York and maintain my family connections in the center of the state. Overseeing exams provided a three-day holiday from the phone and my practice. While our normal board service accommodations were rather austere, for exams we had a suite in the best hotel, and we wined and dined at the finest restaurants. Even though the small compensation barely covered expenses and didn't begin to make up for our lost income, all the board members were happy to be giving something back to our profession.

Dr. Lee and I grew close. He was also a bird dog enthusiast and trialed some fine dogs. We talked dogs and practice by the hour—he, too, practiced small-animal medicine. Our friendship continued through the years.

The board was often successful in our efforts to prosecute the quacks and to prevent them from doctoring without a license. But then there was Ike Stoltzfus. He was one of the slickest and most elusive. We simply couldn't get anywhere with Ike. Year in and year out he evaded our most skilled investigators. Ike was Amish, and he plied his self-licensed trade among the large, productive farms in the land of the "Plain People" in Lancaster County.

The Amish are interesting people and great farmers. They're called Plain People because of their dark, unadorned clothing. Some of the women wear white or ivory-colored bonnets, but otherwise black or the darkest navy blue is the rule. The married Amishman is always bearded; the single, clean-shaven. They refuse to own tractors or motor-driven equipment. If something isn't mentioned in the Bible, it isn't part of their lives, so horses or mules pull the plow or buggy. Almost all Amish eschew electricity in their homes or barns. The old-

fashioned oil lamp was good enough for Abraham; it is good
enough for them.

These people are against Social Security and believe the
family and community should care for their old and infirm.
They successfully fought in court against mandatory schooling of their children during harvest and planting times. If a
barn or house burns down or needs building, the neighbors
gather and build the family what it needs. Crime is almost
nonexistent. When transgressions occur, they are not made
public. Offenders are punished or disciplined within their
church or community group. The most severe form of punishment is known as shunning. The whole community turns from
the sinner. People neither speak to nor look at the offender. It
is as though the individual doesn't exist. Although the Amish
are rigid, they are a quiet, peace-loving, religious people and
a great community asset.

Ike was the best-known Amish animal doctor in the country. He was a thorn in the side of the local licensed vets, who
filed numerous complaints and simply couldn't understand
why we hadn't taken legal action to stop his flagrant, illegal
doctoring. It was almost a joke. The investigator would dutifully go to a farmer and tell him he knew Ike was treating the
farmer's stock. Being one of the brethren, the farmer wanted to
protect Ike, yet the Amish are not supposed to lie. "Ya, I do
recollect he was here." The investigator would press: "We
know he treated a cow of yours with milk fever and that you
paid him. He has no license." The farmer's memory would always become clouded at this point. "Ya, now, maybe we did
give a little present for his advice. Could be a ham or something."

There was just no way the Amish farmers would testify
against Ike. He was well liked and a deacon or something
similar in the church. His fees were well below those of a licensed vet, and he occasionally did pro bono work. He also
bartered, a common practice among the Amish. The Amish
have their own laws and live separately within the larger com-

munity. Their refusal to acknowledge the legitimacy of the Pennsylvania state government's right to license who would give their animals medical care had a certain logic to it and fit with their strict moral code.

Frustrated and tired of being told how derelict and ineffectual we were, we became desperate to "get Ike" and even discussed sending an investigator disguised as an Amishman. The chief investigator laughed at the suggestion. "What are you talking about? They all know each other. A stranger would be spotted right off. Besides, the attorney general would veto it as possible entrapment."

So year in, year out, we could feel the old fox thumbing his nose at us. When I left the board, his file was still open, three inches thick and labeled "under investigation." That was untrue. The investigators had long since given up. For all I know, one of Ike's sons or grandsons is still doctoring. The Amish adhere to tradition and usually do what their predecessors did before them. In many ways, they might be right. I never heard of a drunken Amishman killing a family with his horse and buggy. They have never bred a known serial killer. An Amish jail, at most a four-cell, is never full, while one of our most flourishing industries is building new prisons.

To my great sadness, Dr. Stader succumbed to his coronary problems during my tenure on the state board. His internship program never made it out of committee, but somehow that didn't seem to matter. His crown of accomplishments needed no further stars. He had been a helpful, powerful force in my professional life. I will always miss him.

seventeen

A Most Mysterious Case

My practice was flourishing at the time I saw one of the most puzzling cases of my career. During office hours patients were booked about twenty minutes apart. That allowed ample time, especially for routine follow-ups such as ear cases and vaccinations—a far cry from the days when I sat idly, hoping for a new owner or patient to wander in. It also permitted me time for a very occasional coffee or soda break, or a few minutes to walk around the hospital to stretch my legs.

Mrs. Walsh approached me on such a break. "Your next case is a referral from Dr. Huggler." She glanced at the patient card. "He couldn't find any physical reason for the problem. He thinks it's a possible behavioral case, a possible vice, like tail chasing." On rare occasions, Dr. George Huggler, a fine local vet and a friend, sent me a referral, as I did him, when a client wanted another opinion.

"So . . ." I looked at Mrs. Walsh, certain more was coming.

"Your patient is a five-year-old male castrated golden retriever."

Knowing her, and having some time to spare, I indulged her desire for drama. "What else?"

"The owner, Mr. Winston, is one of the most handsome men I've ever met." She was almost gushingly girlish. "He's about my age, beautifully spoken, and very knowledgeable."

I grinned. "About your age?" Like Jack Benny, Mrs. Walsh was a perennial thirty-nine and would never divulge her age—never had a birthday.

"Doctor, don't joke. His dog is a Seeing Eye dog. Mr. Winston is blind, so sad." She brightened. "Can you believe he writes children's books in Braille?" My interrogator-secretary had been at work. This could go on and on.

I looked at my watch. "Well, send them into the exam room." This would be a very interesting case. George Huggler seldom missed. He was a good diagnostician.

The patient, a good-looking, oversized, and somewhat overweight golden, entered first. The owner followed. Mr. Winston had a firm grip on the Seeing Eye's harness. He introduced himself and his other companion, a man considerably younger. "Dr. Scanlon, this is Bill Duncan, my chauffeur and Seeing Eye human, and of course you know all about Milton, my dog."

I shook the offered hands, including Milton's paw, and took this opportunity to study Mrs. Walsh's "most handsome" man. She wasn't far off the mark. He looked to be in his late forties, with chiseled, perfect features. He was tall and slender, with a head of dense, graying hair and a thin, steel-colored, neatly trimmed mustache. His dark glasses were small, and his explosive, almost penciled eyebrows were quite visible. His muscular arms and shoulders stood out through his lightweight summer shirt. Indeed, he was an impressive-looking man.

"Let me review Dr. Huggler's findings for a moment. I've got his complete report here." George, as usual, had been thorough. His examination showed no physical reason why Milton would occasionally jump forward, as described by Mr. Winston.

"Mr. Winston, tell me about his forward jumping. Dr. Huggler describes it as a lunging or twisting motion."

"Well, as you know, he guides me through the harness grip. Now and then he'll lunge forward, kind of jump. I get a false signal. It's very confusing, and it disturbs my confidence and trust." He paused. "He's highly trained and has been most reliable until the past month or so. He's really a dear, and we're a good team. He's opened the world back up for me. I thought I had lost it." He paused again. "The question is, is it something physical or a bad habit that he developed? Dr. Huggler is stymied."

"Well, sometimes two heads are better than one. Let me examine Milton," I suggested. Privately, I wasn't optimistic. George Huggler was very competent.

As I expected, Milton was no help, although in his friendly golden retriever way, he tried his best. His reflexes were perfect. There was a small amount of excessive wax in his ears. "Does he lean forward, then stop and scratch his ears?" I asked.

"No, it's not accompanied by any scratching."

I continued to examine my patient slowly, stalling for time as I tried to visualize this vague "forward thrust or lunge" and trying to think of what might prompt such an action. Careful palpating and gentle squeezing of almost every inch of his body elicited no sensitive area. In no way did he resent my probings. Milton was a very calm, cool, sensible dog.

I carefully checked his harness and the body areas it touched. Nothing abnormal or even suspicious. Nothing that might cause so much as a twinge of discomfort, let alone a forward lunge.

Dr. Stader's advice came to mind: "Eliminate the commonplace causes first, then look for the exotic." There was nothing commonplace. Exotic? A brain tumor? No way. No symptoms whatsoever. But certainly something physically wrong was causing his bizarre actions. He was not the least bit high-strung and showed no signs of nervous vices. Besides, Seeing Eye dogs were carefully chosen before their very long and intensive training period. Any bizarre behavior would have been weeded out early on.

At this point I had no clue. I was nowhere near a diagnosis.

"Mr. Winston, can you tell me anything you may have overlooked in your description of this problem? Is there any pattern? Does it occur at certain times or in certain places? Under similar conditions?" I was still stalling, trying to get more information.

He hesitated thoughtfully before answering. "No. It is purely random. It's happened in different places and times. I've tried to relate it myself, but there is no pattern. I wish he could talk. He'd tell us." Mr. Winston stopped, cutting off his words. "How stupid of me. I forgot to mention that sometimes I've heard his teeth click." He paused. I waited. "These episodes are rare, but rethinking, I have heard a clicking each time." He stroked his chin several times. Under the bright examination room lights, I noticed a lighter skin tone on his chin. Mr. Winston had, I guessed, recently shaved off a goatee, or was it misapplied make-up?

It is interesting how some small, seemingly unimportant nugget of information or some forgotten experience can lie dormant in one's mind. It is fascinating how it can spring to life and come back to you when properly stimulated. The "teeth clicking" was my stimulant. It brought to mind the picture of a snapping or biting dog. It also reminded me of a long-forgotten description of a condition called muscae (for *flies*) volitantes, where the animal snaps at imaginary flies. This condition is not recognized as an entity in today's literature. I can't tell you what memory synapses fired in my brain to pull it out.

This condition occurs when the fluid portion of the eye, the vitreous humor, contains a small cyst or cysts, or some precipitated protein particles. These small bodies occasionally float across the visual area. The dog sees what appears to be a fly or gnat and snaps at the moving object. In snapping, he lunges forward to some degree. A blind man's sensitive hands could easily perceive the thrust as a jump or lunge.

I sighed slightly. Mr. Winston's keen ears picked it up. "Oh, my." He drew up his hand with drooping fingers. "Does that mean you're stumped, too?"

Sighing again, I answered, "No. It means that I think I might have found the cause. I'm going to reexamine his eyes." Going back to the ophthalmoscope, I carefully checked Milton's eyes. I wasn't certain, but I thought I detected some small opalescent bodies in the forepart of the eyes.

Mrs. Walsh's "Mr. Handsome" listened carefully as I explained what little I knew of the rare condition. "So, with my limited knowledge I can't offer any treatment or even a positive diagnosis. I can only make a tentative diagnosis, and since it might impair Milton's usefulness as a guide dog, I want to be wrong." By now, Mr. Winston was seeking comfort from his companion, Mr. Duncan, who was hugging his friend and murmuring sympathy. "Don't despair," I encouraged. "There might be answers I don't have."

During this era in veterinary medicine, many specialists were appearing, especially at the nearby vet school at the University of Pennsylvania. "I can't really help Milton, Mr. Winston, but there is an eye specialist I'm going to refer you to who probably can. I think you'll feel better with a specialist who does nothing but canine ophthalmology." I gave them a referral letter and with that, the trio departed, comforting one another with obvious strong affection. There was no satisfaction for me in this case.

Mrs. Walsh would surely be after me before the next patient. I was ready.

"Well?" she questioned.

"Yes, handsome." I looked ceiling-wise. "But I don't see any future for you. You met Mr. Duncan."

She tossed her head, handing me the next patient's history card. "In some ways, you're as bad as Dr. Stader." I looked at her back. As usual, she had the last word.

The specialists at the University of Pennsylvania confirmed my diagnosis, and it did indeed end Milton's usefulness as a guide dog. He remained, however, with Messrs. Winston and Duncan as a much-beloved pet. He got along well with the new guide dog, and caring for those two selfless, majestic, calm dogs, and observing the steadfast relationship of their owners, was my pleasure for many years.

eighteen

Tales from the Cat House

As my practice grew, I noticed there were more and more cats as pets. Fifty years ago, cats were scarce in a veterinarian's office. People resented having to spend their hard-earned money on an animal that just strayed into their yard and came and went as it pleased. With the advent of more women working outside the home, cats began to gain in popularity until currently they outnumber dogs in many practices. Cats are not very demanding, but they fill a household with affection and humor.

Although I would have to call myself a dog person, I enjoy cats and am often amazed at the variety of their personalities. I have enormous admiration for their adaptability; they are equally at home in a one-room apartment or a hundred-acre farm. I think what I enjoy most about them, though, is their apparent duality. No other animal is so domesticated on the outside yet so wild on the inside. A cat can be a purring, well-fed pet dozing on a lap one minute, and with the proper stimulus, can be transformed into a stalker of prey, a merciless killer, the next minute.

As my practice grew beyond my ability to handle the number of clients I had, I hired associates. My problem became how to keep them. The good ones wanted what I had: the independence of one's own business, where one's talent and hard work were for self and family. It always reached a point where additional salary increases were no incentive. They wanted to go out on their own, and who could blame them? Unfortunately, they always took some clients with them. Most of these vets were fine, well-adjusted, capable people.

One of the very best was Dr. Robert Barndt. Bob was an ex–football player who might have made the big time if it weren't for a bad shoulder. A big man who carried his weight well, he looked the part. He had receding, dark hair and huge, huge hands. How he managed some of our exceedingly delicate surgeries was beyond me, but he was a whiz. I related well to Bob and liked his family of three great kids. His wife, Kay, was something special.

I knew he wasn't going to remain with me once his contract expired. I didn't want to lose him—I had been looking for someone special like him to move with me to my next level of growth. I devised what I hoped was the proverbial offer you can't refuse.

"Bob, stay with me another year. Meanwhile, we'll look for a location and together design and build the finest and most modern hospital on the Main Line. I'll supply most of the financing and guarantee your salary during the lean front years. We'll be equal partners, with a buy-out option after seven years."

His desire to practice with only the best equipment, in the finest facility, won out. He knew he was in no financial position to build such a facility himself, and so Devon Animal Hospital was born. It was a beautiful, state-of-the-art hospital across the road from the nationally famous Devon Horse Show grounds on Lancaster Avenue in Devon, Pennsylvania.

Before Bob left for Devon, I was fortunate to contract for the services of the outstanding Dr. Lillian Guiliani to replace him. She was one of the first lady veterinarians of that time and is still, at this writing, in active practice—for herself, naturally.

Bob and I had minor differences of opinion over the hospital design but were in complete accord on the "Cat House." With the ever-increasing percentage of cat patients in the practice, we were determined to provide the absolute finest in deluxe accommodations and feline care. The Cat House, while attached to the main hospital, was a separate wing so the dogs wouldn't disturb the cats with smell or sound. Each pen was oversized and contained a big loafing perch, a window, and a small, non-toxic tree. The cats also enjoyed soft music playing constantly. We were extremely pleased, and so were our cat-owning clients. By the end of our first year, the Cat House was always filled, and we had a waiting list for boarders.

Dr. Barndt ran the Devon hospital. I occasionally helped with surgery but mainly spent my time at my Narberth Animal Hospital. We met often for lunch, during which he would relate Cat House stories. "Bob," I once remarked, "I hope we have some canine patients, too."

"Yeah, yeah, but let me tell you about the three cats I got last week." Bob was a true cat fancier and preferred them to dogs. "There was a lady, a recluse, lived in a little house. She took an overdose because she had cancer. Amazingly, she wrote a note to send the cats here to be boarded and cared for indefinitely. She was very wealthy." He had his trump card ready. "Now how do you suppose she knew about the Cat House? She wasn't a client."

"How, Bob?" I had best get this over with.

"She called the township's animal control officer and asked where the finest facility in the state was!"

I understood Bob's pride. There had been a lot of sweat starting the practice, and a lot of financial risk. The Cat

Edward J.
Scanlon

House could have been an expensive flop, but our best judgment had told us otherwise. Thankfully, we were vindicated, and it helped get us out of the red during that start-up period when clients were few. I had been there before!

Bob always had numerous cat stories that I tolerated and pretended interest in for the sake of our friendship, but most of them were boring. Being called by the township manager about how to get a cat down from a power line safely was not my idea of excitement or feline medicine. There was one occasion, though, when he called me about a cat, and I hung on his every word.

"We are in deep doo-doo, Ed, big trouble." It took him quite a while to give me the details. At his conclusion, I agreed we were in deep doo-doo. There was a possibility of a lawsuit we couldn't win. More important, though, Devon Animal Hospital's reputation could be seriously damaged, as could that of its directors. We knew of veterinarians whose images had been damaged by the press because of a mistake. This was an honest mistake, but nevertheless it was clear negligence.

Despite the superstition that black cats bring bad luck (which I was tempted to agree with by the end of this episode), many owners kept and loved them. There were several that were boarded at the Cat House. Somehow, one of them, appropriately named Satan, was given by mistake to a young couple who came to pick up their black cat. Satan was placed in their cat carrier by our staff, and the carrier was handed to the couple. Off they went, in a big hurry, with the wrong cat.

About a week later, Satan's true owners arrived to retrieve their beloved pet. Mr. and Mrs. Stallinger were an older, childless couple who proved the axiom that people who are together for years grow to look like each other. They were thin and gray of hair, complexion, and clothing. They immediately realized that the black cat given to them was not theirs. The kennel person on duty came to Bob, very upset. "This is the only black cat in the hospital. They say it isn't their Satan."

Bob investigated and, after much detective work, realized what had happened. He explained the mistake to the frowning Mr. Stallinger and his panicked mate. "A young couple, James and Adela Bronson, were given your Satan by mistake. I'll personally go to the Bronson home and retrieve Satan and deliver him to you tonight," Bob promised.

Mrs. Stallinger voiced one of many frightening possibilities. "He might have run away. He wouldn't know their house. They could have turned him out. He's not an outside cat."

Bob was sweating. He realized that something had to be very, very wrong. The Bronsons had not called, asking where their cat was. I could just imagine his worry, which had now become mine. But the worst was yet to come. Bob went to the young Bronsons' home. It was empty, with a big "Sold" sign planted on the front lawn.

The neighbors were of little help. The Bronsons had lived there for only a year and were private, even unfriendly. At this point, the Stallingers were becoming a little nasty and threatening. Who could blame them!

"Give the Stallingers the facts and hire a detective," I advised. "You still have a hospital to run. Show them you are doing everything possible. Try to be optimistic and keep their hopes up." Thus, Bob had the additional embarrassment of explaining to a detective "The Case of the Missing Cat."

Within a day the detective reported yet another problem. He had found and contacted Mr. Bronson's new employer and obtained the couple's new apartment address and phone number in Cincinnati, Ohio. Unfortunately, they didn't answer the phone. "I'll keep calling. Maybe I'll reach them tonight. I'll call you when I do, no matter how late," the detective promised. I often thought later that I would enjoy hearing his version of this story.

Near midnight he found them at home, only to discover that they had taken the cat to the Chester County SPCA. "What with moving to a smaller apartment and the new job, they just couldn't handle a pet," the detective explained. "So they made the decision, prior to picking up the cat at your hospital, that they would take it to the SPCA. They never even opened the carrier. They just handed the container to the clerk."

We were in a panic. At 7:30 A.M. the next morning, Bob was at the SPCA waiting for the doors to open. The big worry, of course, was that after the holding period, if no adoption took place, the society had the right to euthanize, and black cats were not in demand. It was a nightmare.

Bob was spared a possible heart attack. Satan had been adopted. The name and address of the adopting party were furnished. The next hurdle was to convince Satan's new family to return him to his loving kingdom. I still don't know how Bob convinced them, but I suspect it involved some free veterinary service. Over the years, Bob had many more tales from the Cat House for me, but none of them rivaled the experience with Satan Stallinger.

Like his partner, Bob has been retired for some years, and enjoys his home at the Jersey shore. Devon Animal Hospital is still flourishing and still known for its fine cat facilities.

Searching my memory and my many experiences for dramatic or riveting feline stories has been fruitless. Cats don't meow loudly enough to warn of a burglar or fire. Their survival kit doesn't permit them to face snowstorms in search of lost travelers or to plunge into icy lakes to rescue their owners. They refuse to herd or guard man's flocks or cattle. They do defend granaries, homes, and barns against rodents, but there is little romance in that. Their sheer numbers as pets and fireside companions attest to a different kind of success, however. Apparently all they have to do to be loved is be themselves—just cats. Who can argue with many centuries of success?

nineteen

BAB—a Most Unusual Man

What kind of man drops out of high school, starts his career as a taxi driver, and ends up a multimillionaire dog food manufacturer? What sort of man can sell his company for many millions and still retain ownership of its manufacturing plants and warehouses? What kind of man would refuse to spend a penny on TV, radio, or print ads after his ad agency shows a direct correlation between such ads and growing sales charts?

Such a man could well be named Mr. Unusual, but his name actually was Bernard A Bernard. Originally it was Bernard A Fagleman. He didn't like his last name, so why not have the same first and last name? The *A*, I learned, stood for nothing. "It just supports the Bs," he told me. Again, unusual, but that was the way he thought—just a little differently than you or I would.

BAB introduced himself to me, early in my career, as the president of Trim Dog Food Company. His card failed to mention that he was also plant manager, purchasing agent, chief salesman, financial officer, and on occasion, butcher. After a firm handshake, the wide-shouldered man announced, "Doc, you get a free meat freezer, twice-a-week delivery, emergency delivery at any time. You are guaranteed the freshest diced horse meat at the lowest price. You're billed every two weeks and can deduct two percent for payment within ten days."

I liked this man's approach. Direct, and without the usual compliments about the hospital or my profession. His delivery was friendly, although there was a little wariness in the cool blue eyes. He was ready to gossip and exchange jokes like any good salesman, but his prospects determined the meeting's flavor.

At that time, my boarding wing for pets was becoming quite busy. The Main Line residents with high spendable income took many lengthy vacations without their pets. Fortunately, many of them had come to depend on me to provide care. The "house diet" at that time, fed to boarders and patients alike, was basically a good-quality dry kibble mixed with cooked meat and gravy to make it palatable and attractive. This was in the days before the excellent commercial foods were readily available. (Of course, some sick animals required special diets.) The meat—beef—was the most expensive part of the diet.

While the idea of horse meat was slightly repellent, its low cost, low fat content, and high pet acceptance were causing it to be widely used in kennels and hospitals. I agreed to give it a trial. It worked out well, and I became a Trim customer.

Several weeks later, on a Thursday, BAB invited me to lunch. It was pleasant, and we hit it off on many subjects. This invitation was repeated every few weeks until eventually we met almost every Thursday, hundreds of lunches spanning decades of friendship. We become confidants and I became an unpaid (except for free horse meat) but not unappreciated Trim Dog Food consultant.

At that time, Trim horse meat was processed in a small

building in West Philadelphia and then delivered from house

to house, from hospital to kennel by a fleet of Jeeps. Bernie had acquired a Jeep agency headquartered in Ardmore, Pennsylvania, which sold Jeeps and serviced his fleet at minimal cost. Logical and cost-effective. Typical BAB thinking.

One Thursday, many years into our friendship, he dropped a bomb. "I'm considering giving up my retail customers and Jeep delivery. I'm going into canning. That way, I can expand my product line and reduce costs per unit. I can eliminate a lot of billing and headaches. What do you think?"

I threw up my hands. "Slow down, Bernie. I need time to think. Order another martini.

"Now you have a sure thing, Bernie. You're making money. If you do this, you'll be fighting the biggest dog food manufacturers in the country for supermarket and store shelf space. Besides, you don't know a damn thing about a canner."

I paused, and smiled at my friend. I was reminded of Roy Davis trying to dissuade me from leaving the safety of DuPont. Bernie had already made up his mind. His question was only a courtesy. "Good luck, Bernie. You've made up your mind." I had some doubts, though. Purina, Alpo, and others had created the pet food market and would be mighty adversaries.

He grinned. We understood each other. "Ed, you're going to be a part of it. You're coming aboard as a poorly paid consultant. I have to formulate new products and if the dogs and cats don't like them, they won't eat them. If they won't eat, neither will Reba and the kids." Like my family, BAB's was growing and eating, eating, eating. "That's your job, Ed. Come up with something they will eat."

Briefly, he borrowed a large sum of money, rented a huge plant ("We'll have room to grow," he told me), and called in the can company's agents, who helped set up the canning line and the machinery. We had fun formulating and naming the new products. Bernie, of course, did the unusual once again. "The Cadillac name is synonymous with quality. We are now the Cadillac Dog Food Company, no longer Trim." When the Cadillac Motor Company lawyers threatened suit and demanded he desist in the use of their name, he simply advised them they should be honored he had chosen their name and not Plymouth or Chrysler. "After all, if your customers are confused between your cars and our dog food, you don't want them anyway." The lawyers went away.

One of our big hits was the so-called Cadillac 5 in 1 formula. This consisted of chicken, liver, beef, lamb, and cereals. To increase the profit, there were only token amounts of beef and lamb. We included liver in all formulas, at my insistence. "If they don't eat it, the owner doesn't ever buy it again," I reminded him. "Liver has appeal to all dogs and cats. Plus, it's fairly cheap."

For our local, established customers, we kept Cadillac Trim Horse Meat in the product line. We had several Cadillac Puppy Food formulas and one for kittens. We pioneered a reducing diet for obese pets long before the "big boys" tapped into that market.

It was hard sledding the first year, but Bernie somehow had Cadillac Dog Food in most of the major chain food stores and numerous small independents by the second year. The company began to show profits, then big profits, and eventually huge profits. Bernie no longer rented. He owned a monster plant in Camden, New Jersey.

There was very little regulation of the canned pet food industry at that time. Aside from listing the protein, fat, and carbohydrate percentages and their sources, the industry disclosed very little. The water content in all formulas was quite high. Bernie was fond of saying, "We get more money for an ounce of liquid than the liquor industry."

Cadillac products were very competitive, and Bernie spent a large amount on advertising, especially in the first few years. I recall one year when BAB was quite upset with his advertising agency. "Can you imagine, Ed, they insisted, almost demanded, I budget a million dollars for TV, newspapers, radio, and whatnot for next year's campaign?" He was cross. "Just because they show a chart with advertising

costs going up and sales with it, they tell me I must spend a
million."

I was interested, waiting for what I knew would be another
BAB Unusual approach. "What did you tell them?"

He laughed and patted his pants pocket. "I told them the
million was going in my pocket. That makes me a millionaire.
I was a taxi driver and they just fulfilled my ambition. I fired
them and they're not getting a cent."

I knew my buddy. "Come on. What are you really going to
do?"

He was warmed up. "Ed, I just rented a dozen white con-
vertible Cadillacs and hired a dozen lovely ladies. We fill the
Caddys up with Cadillac Dog Food products and the ladies
will give them away at supermarket parking lots, stores, any-
place. I'm making similar arrangements in New York, Baltimore, and Washington, since they're our major markets."

"Won't people without pets get cans?" I was skeptical of
his abandonment of conventional advertising.

He was enthused. "They'll give them to friends who have
pets." He paused, a shadow crossing his face. "It will be
used." It was sad but true. Cadillac Dog Food sold extremely
well in poor areas where there were relatively few pets. We
both agreed it was excellent nutrition, and that we would
rather see poor children eat a well-balanced dog food than fill
up with junk foods. At least they were getting protein.

His campaign was a huge success. It received a lot of free
TV coverage and press pictures. It cost a lot less than the million the ad agency had insisted was needed, and sales continued to go up. Of course, it was a great one-time gimmick, and
he returned to conventional advertising the next year. You can
imagine how chastened his agency was when he rehired them,
and I suspect they never again told him what he *had* to do.

Bernie and I were close socially as well. His wife and mine
were very compatible and my girls were extremely fond of
Uncle Ben and Aunt Ree, looking forward to their visits with
anticipation. Ben and his wife, Reba, had married when they

were barely sixteen. Maryland permitted marriage at that age then, and they secretly eloped. He often said, "We were born married."

They married so young and saw all life had to offer together. He drove a taxi the first two years of their marriage, and they saved enough to open a delicatessen in Drexel Hill, Pennsylvania, where they lived frugally over the store. He cut fresh meat, and that's how he stumbled into the dog food business. There were many requests from customers for fresh meat scraps for pets, and he recognized a market.

BAB and Reba had gone from rags to riches together. He would tease Reba that she just wasn't spending enough, that she wasn't maintaining her quota. She would look at him with a smile and tell him she had everything she needed. Her look said it all. Bernie and I attended many field trials together, fished off his yacht in later years, and traveled together. I never saw him show the slightest interest in any other woman. He was truly well and happily married and still in love with his Reba at his death at age seventy-nine.

Another BAB Unusual was his solution to a production line problem. "Ed, I am stuck. I'm working three shifts and can't get enough production to fill my orders. I've had the canning engineers in for days and they're no help." He was distraught, which was rare.

"What's the problem?"

"When I speed up the canning line, the cans wobble and fall off the belt. We're putting in new machinery and canning lines, but they won't be ready for at least three months. I need to increase production now. When you don't fill orders, you lose customers."

"I'm just your veterinary consultant. I don't have the foggiest," I offered sympathetically. "Maybe the engineers are right. You simply have to wait till the new production equipment kicks in."

Bernie shook his head. He was disturbed. "I can't wait, Ed. There must be an answer." I knew that, with his quirky intelligence, if there were an answer, he would find it and it would be unusual.

A day later he called me, his tone triumphant. "I told you there was an answer. It's simple." He went on to describe his solution, and it *was* simple, a "blinding glimpse of the obvious." "I put magnets under the metal can belting. That holds them down so they can't wobble and fall off. I can increase output ten percent and that solves the problem."

Most people would have accepted the engineers' verdict. After all, they were the pros. BAB remarked, "Maybe it's just as well I didn't get a higher education. I'm too dumb to know it can't be done." As usual, he was right!

We were close, so I especially missed his company when he became a yacht owner. He studied navigation until, in true BAB fashion, he was able to fire his captain and take over as the master of the *Brimful,* his state-of-the-art, 60-foot luxury vessel. I didn't begrudge him his pleasure, but I missed his company. He spent his winters in the Bahamas and the Caribbean, during which time he ran Cadillac Dog Food Company by ship's telephone. (How he would have loved today's fax machines, e-mail, and conference calls.) Summers he returned to his beautiful Kimberton, Pennsylvania, farm and sailed the Chesapeake Bay.

Bernie's ultimate Unusual coup occurred when he sold his Cadillac Dog Food Company to U.S. Tobacco Company. During a Thursday lunch, he raised his martini in salute and said, "We have been close and you've helped me make Cadillac a success. The big payoff is about to come, and I want you to benefit."

Of course, I was interested. "What big payoff?" His terse statement was a complete surprise. I had had no clue.

"You know I've had many offers to buy Cadillac, and I've decided to sell. U.S. Tobacco will pay top dollar." Certainly he had told me of the offers he received, but he had never indicated any interest.

I was surprised and voiced a thought. "What will you do? You sure don't need any more money!"

"Ed, look at me. Look at yourself. You've forgotten. We've been palling around, playing and working hard together for darn near thirty-five years. I've accomplished more than I ever dreamed. I'm tired. I want out." He smiled and laid a hand over mine. "We're the same, but we're different. All I wanted was to make money. You love your work and I've always envied you that. I've never loved Cadillac. It's adios time.

"The terms of sale will show, in a small way, my appreciation of your help. It certainly can't cover my affection. You're to remain on as consultant for three years at a hefty salary." He smiled. "Of course, you'll actually do little or no work. They have their own experts."

I was touched. But once again, I realized how little insight we truly have into people, no matter how close we are. I never suspected that Cadillac Dog Food Company was just a money-making vehicle to Bernie. I always thought it was a love.

Settlement with U.S. Tobacco, to which I was invited, took place at their corporate headquarters in New York. Everything went smoothly until signature time. BAB rose and announced there would be one small change needed before he signed.

The tobacco president spoke. "We've all worked on this for over six months. What the hell is the small change?" I pitied him. If he had been working on this with BAB for six months, he was close to being a broken man. He just didn't know it yet.

Bernie explained. "Everything will remain as is, but my heirs (or I, if I am still alive) will regain ownership of the manufacturing plants and warehouses in twenty years, sans equipment. Meanwhile, I will lease them to you for one dollar a year for twenty years. Simply put, the real estate then reverts back to me or my heirs."

Bernie sat down and observed the inevitable explosion. The president screamed, the chief accountant hollered, the three vice presidents all carried on in unison. Finally they wore down.

The president took over. "This is ridiculous. You're getting millions and we won't even own the plants and warehouses? You're crazy. No way."

BAB rose again. "Look around this table. All of you U.S. Tobacco people will be retired in ten years, fifteen at the most. You're only buying Cadillac because it will make money for you. You'll still get it. That's what you really bought. You're not buying Cadillac for buildings or real estate."

There was a lot more noise and loud arguments. BAB suggested, "Let's break for lunch. You people talk it over. Give me your answer by two-thirty today. There will be no sale unless you agree to this most reasonable and inconsequential change."

I hadn't made a sound. I could hardly believe his ultimatum, and I was used to his outrageous ideas and demands. The baldness of his position and his business insight—a most unusual concept from a most unusual man. From my standpoint, and his as well, I hoped they accepted it.

It took them a week but U.S. Tobacco Company, under protest, finally bought Cadillac Dog Food Company sans the plants and warehouses. They did have a nice one-dollar-a-year lease for twenty years.

Bernie was a great believer in education, and as usual, he was willing to put his money where his mouth was. He donated almost $2 million to Dickinson University in Carlisle, Pennsylvania, to build the Bernard and Reba Bernard Center for the Study of the Humanities. I often wonder if the hundreds of students who have been educated there have any idea of what their benefactor was like. Certainly not like any other millionaire they might ever meet. I hope a touch of his creativity and genius for the unusual passes to them.

Bernie was my great and true, close friend for many years. I still miss him. Many times, though, I feel his presence. Sometimes I ask him what I should do in uncertain business situations. He often has an unusual solution, and it invariably works.

twenty

Dog Show Days

Have you ever attended a dog show? If not, see one at your first opportunity. Even if your canine affection level is cool to neutral, you will enjoy yourself. Having attended two large outdoor shows yearly, as official vet, for decades, I can attest to the pleasure most spectators experience. Since parking and admission usually are not prohibitive, it makes an economical family outing. Most children love dog shows. They are entranced and amazed at the variety of man's best friend.

An official veterinarian must be present at all accredited American Kennel Club (AKC) shows. He or she is available for emergency care such as fight wounds, accidents, or heatstroke and to serve as arbitrator or confirm a judge's decision that could eliminate a contestant. For example, a lame dog is considered unsound. Sometimes the lameness is barely visible. The judge will, on occasion, call on the vet to confirm the judge's edict that the dog should not be shown.

Mostly, however, the vet sits in a tent or official station and reads the newspaper and show catalogue, sipping coffee or a cold drink and chatting with dog handlers, officials, and members of the public who want some information or directions. Although an information booth is available, people seem to prefer the vet, expecting his or her knowledge to extend even to the whereabouts of the bathrooms. The vet will talk with clients who are exhibiting their dog or dogs, always wishing them luck. Since the dogs shown come from all over the country, there is not much client contact.

An outdoor dog show at which I officiated for many years was the Devon Dog Show. It was held on the famous Devon Horse Show grounds, right across the street from my Devon Animal Hospital, and was organized and staged by a group of women with enormous energy and talent. Most of them were Main Line dog breeders, fanciers, and socialites. The profits were donated to the local Bryn Mawr Hospital. Although I was not privy to their financial books, I suspect their profits were small. They held numerous organizational luncheons and dinners and entertained the judges royally, hosting a bang-up party at the show's conclusion. It was a classy show, with many niceties that only ladies can provide. The table at my station always had fresh flowers, a touch I had at no other show. I was also presented with a beribboned bottle of champagne and numerous thank-you kisses from relaxed and happy lady sponsors at show's end. For me these were golden, pleasurable, fun days, and it never rained!

But things were not always as golden as they seemed on the surface. To understand some of the skullduggery, you need a brief and simplified course on how a dog show works.

Let's say you are the loving owners of Our Family's Woofie, a miniature dachshund. In order for Woofie to become an AKC Champion, he must accumulate fifteen points. The number of points awarded at each show differs, depending on the number of dogs entered. Woofie will enter the ring with all the other non-champion male doxies and the judge will pick the one he or she feels most closely resembles the ideal miniature dachshund. The dogs are not so much compared with each other as they are compared with that mental ideal. This is a subtle concept, but it will be important later.

If Woofie wins Winner's Dog (which is how the dog winning the points is designated), then he will move to the next level of competition, Best of Breed. This is where the top-level competition begins. The general public thinks that becoming a champion is the end of the road, but for the true fancier and breeder, it is just the beginning. Champions are fairly common, but the higher ranks are slim indeed.

In Best of Breed, the Winner's Dog and Winner's Bitch re-enter the ring along with all the dogs who are already champions. After careful consideration, the judge will choose the dog that looks the best that day. This dog will be awarded Best of Breed and will move on to Group.

The many breeds recognized by the AKC are organized into seven groups. Let's say Woofie was very, very good today, and won Best of Breed. He would now join the other BOBs from each of the many toy breeds in the Toy group. The judging in Group is more difficult, because it requires the judge to have a mental image of the ideal for each breed, and compare eighteen or nineteen dogs, each of a different breed, with its breed standard rather than with each other. And finally, the best of each group will join for the final competition, Best in Show. This is the most coveted designation of all.

To a large extent, judging dogs on conformation, or beauty, is subjective. Most of the dogs shown are outstanding representatives of their breeds. One judge might eliminate a dog as a contender because to his eye, the neck is a trifle too thick. To another eye, it could be perfect. There is no argument with the judge; his opinion is final.

I enjoyed the beautiful animals in the wonderful spectacle that is a dog show, but sometimes the judges' decisions were suspect. For example, it was hard not to notice that a lady client's boxers always won Best of Breed when I also knew that the judge was her houseguest for an entire week. Certain

prominent professional handlers' dogs often won over what I
considered equal or superior specimens handled by amateur
owners. Judges are rated by how large an entry they draw, and
a handler will bring a dozen or more dogs of clients to show,
while an amateur will bring only one or two.

I was more interested in the other type of class held: not
the beauty contestants shown in Conformation, but the obedience dogs. If an obedience dog refused a command, or performed reluctantly or sloppily, it was obvious. The handler's
social connections were immaterial. I also enjoyed watching
man and dog working in a team, as the dog was born to do.
Non-competitors have never experienced the pleasure and
closeness that develop between dog and owner or handler in
the obedience ring. It would be difficult to decide who gets
the most enjoyment from the adventure.

Throughout my dog show years, it was apparent how
fiercely some owners and handlers competed for the non-cash
prizes, the ribbons, the trophies, and the titles. I saw one case
of competition that involved fraud. The episode involved a
champion collie named Royal Consort. He had won countless
BOBs, and many, many Group firsts, but never the holy grail
of Best in Show. At Devon this particular year, he was again a
finalist for Best in Show.

The judge was an elderly, highly respected gentleman from
California who was known for his feisty and no-nonsense attitude, as well as for his integrity. He appeared very fit himself
and acted with authority. He seemed taller than he was because of his military bearing, which matched his gray crew
cut and waxed mustache. I can't remember his name.

He directed the handlers to trot their dogs up and down the
strip of red carpet. He would occasionally jog along with one
to see the movement more clearly. This tended to add some
drama to the proceedings.

In a dog show, the judge goes over each dog with his
hands. With so many beautifully groomed and full coats, a
hands-on inspection is needed to determine the quality of the

bone structure underneath. Typically, the judge will start at
the front, introducing himself to the dog. Small breeds are
placed on a table to make the examination easier, but with a
large dog like Royal Consort, the judge just bends down.

Royal Consort's jaws were opened to enable the judge to
check for a proper dental occlusion; no overbites or under-
bites are allowed. The judge then ran his hands over the dog's
shoulders and back to feel for proper angulation and muscular development, as well as to determine if the animal was a
proper weight. Next, he felt the hips for dysplasia, checked
the tail for proper fullness and length, and pushed down on
the hips to check for springiness. Finally, the judge ran his
hands between the dog's rear legs for the usually cursory
check to ensure the dog had two testicles.

The judge seemed to recoil and quickly stood erect from
his stooping position. He backed off several steps from the
champion collie and stared in thought. Since these were the
final moments of the dog show, I had left my tent and was
standing at ringside. I had observed many previous moments
of truth, and I knew something was wrong. I had no idea what,
but there was something troubling in the judge's too-long
stare. Most spectators assumed his immobile scrutiny was the
prelude to his selecting the collie as Best in Show and were
buzzing excitedly.

After another moment of apparent thought, he wheeled and
quickly strode to the trophy table, leaned over, and spoke to
his assistant. Shortly I heard a loudspeaker announcement:
"The show veterinarian is requested to report to the judge at
the Best in Show ring." The buzzing increased several deci-
bels. *What gives?* I thought. This was the first such summons
I had ever received in the final, dramatic moments of selection.

At the ring's entrance, my lapel ID pin was inspected and
the judge's assistant directed me to approach the judge. He
wore a perfectly pressed blue and white seersucker suit and I
was impressed with how, even at day's end, he had managed

to maintain perfect grooming. Surely he had replaced the carnation that gave such a dapper touch to his appearance.

His cool, dignified exterior didn't match his scowl and flushed face. "What's the problem, Judge?" I queried.

Through clenched teeth, he barked, "Check the collie's testicles and report back to me."

Walking across the ring, I felt like an actor on a stage. As I approached the magnificent animal, all ringside chatter and noise died down. *What the hell is going on here?* I wondered. The answer came quickly as I palpated the testicles. One felt normal and yielded very slightly to pressure, as expected of normal tissue. The other was abnormally hard and rocklike.

The condition known as cryptorchid, monorchid, or ridgling sprang to my mind. Such an abnormality would bar a dog from being shown and was the reason the judge checked the testicles to begin with. The condition was considered by many as inherited and transmitted to offspring. It was simply a case of one testicle's being retained in the dog's abdomen. The undescended organ was small and prone to be tumorous. The judge was right. This dog was a monorchid. Someone had implanted an artificial testicle. Wow!

How had this been missed over and over again? This dog was a winner and known throughout the United States as a top collie. The only explanation I could think of was that previous between-the-legs checks had been extremely cursory, with just a glancing touch for a quick count. Dogs don't like their testicles squeezed, so the judges had just passed their hands over quickly. This judge didn't.

To the judge, I quietly confided, "You're right. One's an implant."

Now the fun might begin. Was the dignified but feisty judge going to blow his cool? Would he order the dog and its handler out of his ring? Certainly he was angry and insulted. His facial expression gave a hint of his crossness. The situation had explosive potential. Would we see Best in Show history made?

The handler was in jeopardy of losing his license. He was quite successful and commanded expensive fees. The owner was a wealthy breeder and would certainly be stigmatized, no matter what.

Monorchids could reproduce. Suppose Royal Consort had already sired puppies. Possible lawsuits? A real can of worms here.

My speculation ended. "Dr. Scanlon, you may leave the ring. I will meet with you and George Prendergast, the collie's handler, at your station in a half-hour."

He had short words with the handler and resumed his judging. A pretty smart old guy, I thought, as he announced his Best in Show selection. The winner was a very flashy, great-moving, great-coated springer spaniel named Handsome I Am. Funny, decades later I can still remember the dog's name, but I can't the judge's.

When the three of us met at the appointed time, my respect for the judge increased. He took me aside, out of Prendergast's hearing. "Are you prepared to back up our judgment if he denies any wrongdoing?" he questioned in a low, firm voice.

"Yes, sir," I replied. "I'm the co-owner of Devon Animal Hospital, only across the street from here. We have the finest in X-ray equipment."

"Fine," he continued. "You be quiet. I'll handle the matter."

George Prendergast collapsed under the judge's severe castigation. The handler was denounced as a charlatan, a thief, and a disgrace to his profession, among other nasty adjectives. I empathized a little with George's misery under the relentless tongue-lashing—shades of Mrs. Allesandroni's accusations.

Finally, "Everyone deserves a chance at redemption," said the judge, who was a born-again Christian. "You will retain your license if you do as I direct." Now he quietly reeled off his demands. "Royal Consort will never be shown again. He is not to breed. You may continue to show dogs, but never at a show where I am present, and never in the state of California." George, now trembling and close to tears, eagerly agreed.

The judge concluded, "Prendergast, I hope you can explain these restrictions to the owners' satisfaction. If not, refer them to me, as I will be taking action against them also." He then turned to me with a rather formal bow. "Thank you for your help in this despicable matter." Exit the judge.

Predictably, George's participation at shows gradually diminished and he disappeared completely after a couple of years. Certainly no loss, what with his lack of ethics. I didn't want to admit to myself that he might have had a veterinary accomplice in his failed deception. No, probably some quack. Still, I had learned it was amazing what some people would do for the ribbons, the trophies, and the titles.

My few observations of the rare hanky-panky in the dog show world doesn't change the fact that, overall, its participants are sincere, honorable people. Most of them are as honest as their dogs, and that is pretty darn honest.

I admired and enjoyed the obedience-trained dogs so much that I tried to encourage all my clients to train their pets. Every new client was given an enrollment form for the Philadelphia Dog Training Club. Many caring owners followed my advice over the years and they, as well as their charges, reaped its many benefits. An obedience-trained pet is a pleasure. It is like a well-behaved child, enjoyable to all around, its manners admired. For sure, these dogs are more content, happy, and secure than their untrained, ill-mannered cousins. I donated several of Stratoliner's trophies to the club, which acknowledged my efforts by making me an honorary lifetime member, a membership I enjoyed and prize even today.

twenty-one

Absent Love

My relationship with the Allesandroni family continued with house calls and office calls. My respect and liking for the whole family grew with time. Mrs. Allesandroni and I became comfortable enough with each other that we could laugh about our earlier times, and the judge continued to be a figure of honor whom I could look up to.

Several years later, this fine man was devastated when he lost both his wife and his daughter within months of each other—his wife succumbed to cancer and his daughter was killed in an automobile accident. For a few months the judge lived alone in the big house on Judges' Row—a home I had come to know well from my house calls. When it became too difficult to live with the memories, he sold the house and moved to one of the city's fine residential hotels.

Sadly, the move forced yet another loss on him. The two Dobermans, Delilah and Samson II, could not accompany him to the hotel. He called to ask me if the dogs could board permanently with me. "Those dogs are the only living connection I have to my wife and daughter," he said, explaining why he didn't want me to find another home for them. "I can't bear to part with them, and I'd worry about how they were being treated. This way I can visit them, take them to the park to run on Sundays. We used to enjoy watching them. . . ." His misery, loneliness, and pain were palpable even over the phone. "Even though I can't have them with me, I want them as my family. I know you'll care for them and see they get love and attention every day."

I couldn't deny the judge. After our rocky beginning, his wife had become one of my strongest champions as I built my practice. She had been unfailingly kind and generous to me on my many house calls, always showing concern for her dogs. I also admired the judge enormously and valued the connection he had to my father.

Samson and Delilah moved into the hospital the next week. They were great dogs, and after my wife and I moved to the country, they were frequent weekend visitors. Somehow I felt, as I watched them run and play with my ever-growing family of daughters, that the judge's wife and Angelica would have approved.

Samson and Delilah weren't the only permanent residents at my hospital. Several others were there, and each had an interesting story. One of them was Tina, without a doubt the meanest, nastiest cocker spaniel—maybe the nastiest of *any* breed—I ever encountered. Because of the possibility of transmitting diseases, the dogs weren't allowed to mingle, but I had to be even more careful with Tina. She despised other dogs, as well as humans.

Tina was brought to me on a Sunday afternoon, not by her owner, Ethyl Kravitz, but by Ethyl's legal counsel, who described a sad and gruesome scene. It seemed that on that quiet Sunday morning in the upper-class neighborhood of Wynnewood, a burglar broke into the Kravitz home. He proceeded to destroy Max Kravitz's skull with a hammer, managing to leave not a single fingerprint on it. Despite the fact that Mrs. Kravitz had no known talent for carpentry, her fingerprints were quite evident. The mysterious burglar then apparently drove away without being seen or heard by any of the neighbors, and without taking anything, including Max's wallet and his large diamond ring. Mrs. Kravitz knew nothing of the murder until she woke up several hours later, discovered her "dear Max" lying dead on the kitchen floor, and called the police.

The lawyer told me this story, which didn't make the papers until the next morning, and explained that Ethyl stood accused of her husband's murder. "She says that, since she's falsely accused, her dog's expenses should be handled by the accusers. We don't know yet who will be paying you, but someone will take care of it. Ethyl is appealing to you to take care of Tina until her trial."

I didn't like the dog much, but what could I do but accept. If I refused, who knew what would become of Tina, and I didn't want to force her on another unsuspecting vet. She was installed in the boarding wing of my hospital, with a skull and crossbones and other Danger signs around her. When she was let out for a run in the yard that evening, the first thing she did was leap at me, snapping and growling. She had always given me trouble at routine exams, but things were far worse now that her mistress wasn't there to calm her.

It was almost a year before Ethyl was put on trial, and Tina stayed with me all that time. She always greeted the sight of a human, particularly a male, with a threatening growl or snap, but when someone reached out to touch her she shrank away, cowering at the back of her kennel, still growling.

It became a challenge to me to win her over. During idle moments, which were fortunately becoming fewer and fewer, I tried to gain her confidence. But the best I could do was a truce, and that was by bribing her with goodies such as bits of cooked liver or raw eggs, and I gave up on ever having her affection. She tolerated me, but only barely, and my assistant and kennel help not at all.

When Ethyl came up for trial, it was a very prominent case, involving a very prominent Main Line family. Max's brother was a well-known lawyer, and Max had been a big-time builder. He hadn't built houses, only huge projects like malls, hotels, and large apartment buildings. Ethyl was found guilty of non-premeditated murder and given a life sentence. The trial attracted national media coverage for days.

Looking back with the experience of the world that forty additional years brings (and having had my consciousness raised by close association with four daughters!), I have come to see the incident in another, perhaps clearer, light. I now see that both the human murder and the canine hostility could have been brought about by years of physical and emotional battering. We now know that years of day-in, day-out abuse can foster violence or a nervous breakdown in a human, so why not in a dog? Max Kravitz could have created a hostile, frightened dog, one who constantly awaited the next kick or blow, one who expected violence from everyone but her kind mistress.

I cared for Tina through two more years of appeals, during which Ethyl wrote frequent and pathetic letters, asking how her darling was doing. I always answered with the lie that she was happy and thriving. Sometimes the truth serves no good purpose. I believed Ethyl would be a bit happier believing that although she was in jail, the one creature who loved her without reservation was safe and well. Even though Tina was one of the meanest dogs I ever met, I developed admiration for her as a symbol of courage: a gutsy little creature who, despite abuse and mistreatment, was determined to give back as good as she got. Dogs are not born mean. They are made that way.

Another of my family of orphans was Ronnie, a short-haired English pointer. He began his stay when his owner, Pope Yeatman, Jr., an international mining engineer, brought him in to board for a weekend while he visited the gorgeous widow Mrs. Dewitt Newell. "I'll pick him up Monday or Tuesday," he assured me. "Ronnie just doesn't get along with

Jonathan, Mrs. Newell's boxer." I had my doubts about that—Ronnie seemed so good-tempered he could get along with a mountain lion. "She recommended I bring him to you," Pope added. That made sense. I had boarded Jonathan many times while Mrs. Newell was on vacation.

Monday turned into sixteen years. Pope had received an offer he couldn't refuse—the chance to oversee the exploration and opening of a new mine in Brazil. It turned out to be a three-year challenge. He did return several times to visit Ronnie—and Mrs. Newell. The first time, he apologized profusely for not being able to take Ronnie with him, explaining, "I wouldn't have time to take care of him right, and anyway, the jungle's no place for him. Just take care of him until I get back." Each time, he thought Ronnie looked great, and he willingly and faithfully paid the boarding bill and any small medical bills.

Eventually, Pope stopped coming at all. I found out he had gotten another offer, this time in New Zealand, and also that Mrs. Newell had remarried. His payment came in the mail now, with strange postmarks, but the checks were faithful and good.

We made Ronnie the hospital's unofficial mascot. He had the run of the place and the yard. He received lots of affection and attention, and he was one of my daughters' favorites the times I brought him home. He had such a pleasant disposition that he would allow the girls to dress him up. But his lack of freedom bothered me; he was, after all, a hunting dog and should have had fields to run in and birds to hunt. I wrote Pope, care of the New Zealand mining company, asking if he would like me to find the dog a home on a farm or with a bird hunter. The reply came a month later. No, he was sure he'd be back in a year or so and would be able to take care of his dog again. In the meantime, he hoped Ronnie was well and enclosed the check for another year's board.

This went on for years, until Ronnie, still happy, loved, and pampered by all of the staff, was an old, old dog of almost eighteen. There was no denying the cataracts that clouded his expressive brown eyes or the stiffness in his arthritic joints. He no longer seemed to care much about life—even a bitch in heat elicited no more response from him than a sniff at the air and a feeble twitch of his tail. With all the demands of my now-thriving practice and fast-growing girls at home, I hadn't noticed that Ronnie had become a senior citizen. We had been through a great deal together. We had come full circle.

The day arrived when Ronnie could no longer get up. I asked my assistant, Dr. Deter, to put my old friend down. I just couldn't do it. I hadn't cried often in my long career—I couldn't afford to—but this was one of the rare occasions when I couldn't hold back my tears. Ronnie had been such a reliable, cheerful daily presence in our lives, roaming the hospital at will, stopping to put his head in a lap or receive a loving pat, stealing any food we left around, dragging his blanket from place to place.

I tracked Pope Yeatman down in his far-off mine and told him what I had had to do. He surprised me by asking, "Do you think you could send his ashes over here? I'd like to have him with me again." I never thought he cared that much, but love takes many forms. His paying for Ronnie's care all those years, without ever seeing him, without allowing me to give him away, was his own form of love. Absent love of a pet, as shown by Judge Allesandroni, Ethyl Kravitz, and Pope Yeatman, can be far deeper than anyone can imagine.

Today on the grounds of Devon Animal Hospital, near the edge of the woods, stands a small gazebo. This spot is used by clients and staff for private meditation and contemplation. It symbolizes the unbreakable ties of perfect love and pleasure those of us who share our lives with pets experience. I consider myself fortunate that I chose a career that would provide me with happiness and fulfillment.